2023

Writing from Inlandia

AN INLANDIA INSTITUTE PUBLICATION

INLANDIA
INSTITUTE

RIVERSIDE, CALIFORNIA

For more information, write to:
Permissions
Inlandia Institute
4178 Chestnut Street
Riverside, CA 92501

Executive Director: Cati Porter
Publications Coordinator: Laura Villareal
Publications Assistant: Rachel Beronia
Book layout & design: Mark Givens

Printed and bound in the United States
Distributed by Ingram

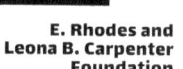

Published by Inlandia Institute
Riverside, California
www.InlandiaInstitute.org
First Edition

2023 Inlandia Creative Writing Workshop Leaders

Alaina Bixon

John Brantingham

José Chávez

Wil Clarke

James Coats

Carlos E. Cortés

Ryan Fingerle

Carlee Franklin

Renee Gurley

Stephanie Barbé Hammer

Bonnie Hearn Hill

Allyson Jeffredo

Caitlyn Johnson

Mae Wagner Marinello

Jerry Mathes

Richard May

Rose Y. Monge

David Puma

Jo Scott-Coe

Frances J. Vásquez

Victoria Waddle

Romaine Washington

This event is supported in part by an award from the National Endowment for the Arts. To find out more about how National Endowment for the Arts grants impact individuals and communities, visit www.arts.gov.

This activity is also supported in part by the California Arts Council, a state agency. Learn more at www.arts.ca.gov.

Contents

My Teachers, the Crows

BY JANET LAKO ALEXANDER

The animals have a lot to teach us
if we just listen,

My uncle always says that.

but I'm still working on
what crows can teach us.

Listen, Uncle!
I think I know
what crows can teach us.

Strut with style!
Glossy black feathers
reflect rainbows
and gleam like jewels.

Don't be afraid to speak up!
Alert your flock
to food or danger.
Raise a ruckus!
Caw, cluck or rattle—
whatever it takes.

Pay attention!
Help your flock
if they get in trouble.
Never forget the face
of someone who helps you.

See, Uncle,
We *can* learn from the crows!
Just like I learn from you.

Mis maestros, los cuervos

BY JANET LAKO ALEXANDER

Los animales pueden enseñarnos mucho
solo tenemos que escuchar,

Mi tío siempre dice eso.

pero todavía trato de descubrir
lo que nos pueden enseñar los cuervos.

¡Oye, Tío!
Creo que sé lo que los cuervos
nos pueden enseñar.

¡Pavonéate con estilo!
Plumas negras y luminosas
reflejan el arco iris
y brillan como joyas.

¡No tengas miedo de hablar en voz alta!
Alerta a tu rebaño
sobre comida o peligro.
¡Arma un alboroto!
Grazna, cloquea o haz un sonido—
haz lo que sea necesario.

¡Presta atención!
Ayuda a tu rebaño
si están en problemas.
Nunca olvides la cara
de alguien que te ayuda.

Mira, Tío,
¡*Sí* podemos aprender de los cuervos!
Tal como yo aprendo de ti.

Why Do I Write?

BY JANET LAKO ALEXANDER

I write for children
to meet them in their world
of dinosaurs, unicorns, and let's pretend
they have little control of their universe
but their imaginations are infinite
and their voices can swell to fill the cosmos

I write for the grown ups, too
Hey, I'm out here
I recognize you
Do you recognize me?

I write for the uncool
the ones who feel too much
the ones who love to laugh at the absurdity
the ones awash in the wonder and sorrow
the ones like you and me

Early 1960s

by Janet Lako Alexander

I remember crawling on a beach towel
spread on spiky green grass
red triangles on white terry cloth
Sailboats, my older sister said

I remember my mother
taking my preschool self outside
to watch a white dot
transit across the mid-morning sky
John Glenn, she said
he's orbiting the Earth

I remember the same sky,
another day
a pilot in a biplane
waving back at my outstretched hand

much like the exuberant sky
in the *Encyclopedia Americana*
year-in-review books,
the color of a Sky Blue Crayola
with stark white rockets
and clouds splashed on it

or the clear Dallas sky
the white of Air Force One
the charcoal and raspberry suits
and roses the color of blood
against an azure backdrop

Secrets

BY MARY BRIGGS

We all have secrets

You and I

Secret things we don't even want to

Tell ourselves

Secrets hidden behind our

Veiled faces

In the deepest recesses of our

Minds

Happenings happened

Deeds done

Words said

Too shameful

Too outrageous

Too hideous

Too horrid

Too embarrassing

Too hurtful

Too heartbreaking

Too different

To share

The Ripper

by Mary Briggs

The Ripper waits for me

I see its shadow on the wall

I hear its footsteps

In the hall

I hear it whisper in my

Ear

My dreamworld it

Invades

I sense it waits just outside

My door

Do I worry?

No

For it is neither

Friend nor foe

It is just

The Ripper

Come what may

It patiently awaits to escort me

Home

Lost

BY MARY BRIGGS

Alas, what troubled days I'm under

Striving to be free

Of all that hampers me

Shed tears

Anguish and lost dreams

The life I love and dread

The dreams I fantasized

Have turned to dust

Scattered by the winds

Of raw reality

Of never-ending doubts

Of regrets and sorrows

Tomorrow a new day begins

The Sarge

BY MARY BRIGGS

War or Peace

He's always there

Like a shepherd among his flock

Leading the way here

Hurrying the rear there

A kind word here

A constructive one there

A smile
A grin
A scowl

A look of approval here

A disdainful there

Tired
Sick
Worn Out

Does his utmost for fatigue not to show

Keeps on leading

Bringing up the rear

Sarge keeps marching on

A MAN among men

Salute to Sarge

The Knitting Woman

BY MARY BRIGGS

I sat across from the knitting woman
As she turned a few strands of yarn into usefulness
To stop a draft
To bundle a child
To give an old man warmth
Her hair was golden white
Framed a halo around her face
Her eyes were twinkling blue
The creases of contentment
showed on her face
Knowing deep down
She was giving love and warmth
To many of Mother Earth's creatures
Who needed love and warmth

The Power of a Tree...

by Stephanie Bruce

It was in the springtime when I came to be. At first, a small and fragile shoot. As the years passed, I grew taller and stronger, all depending upon the water and sunlight given by mother nature that year. One year just as I reached 5 feet tall, there was a terrible freeze. It was so cold for such a long time. It took all my energy to keep myself alive. But in the spring when the sun warmed the earth, I came back strong as ever. I grew a lot that next year.

A man came one day and built a house next to me. I watched as he used wooden beams to hold up his house. I hoped each and every day I would not become one of those beams. Time passed and soon the house was complete. He built a beautiful wooden bench under my grand branches. He brought a woman home. They sat on the bench holding hands. Then one day the man got on his one knee and asked the woman a question. She knocked him over, and screamed, "Yes," as she jumped into his arms.

Then came the child, a little boy. A small and fragile shoot. I watched this small human grow older as I grew taller. He played with a round thing every day on the grass. He bounced it off my trunk. When he was old enough, he climbed up onto my branches. He read books, watched the world go by. Sometimes he even hid from his mom and dad among my branches.

Life went by as I stretched up to the heavens. I watched the little boy become a man. He was all grown up. Soon he left to begin his own life and start his own family. It was on a Sunday when the woman came. She was sitting on the bench under my canopy in the sunlight. She was crying. Then a strange ritual occurred. The next day some men came and dug a large hole underneath my branches. A large wooden box was placed in the hole. I never saw the man again.

Every day the woman came, sat on the bench and talked to the ground, now covered with many flowers. One day she spoke directly to me. She thanked me for always being a constant in their lives. Giving them oxygen, keeping them cool in the hot summer, a place to gather with family, or a place to be alone and quiet, and grow.

The grown man comes with his woman and their children. I watch over them all now. They play in the grass and tend to the flowers and remember the man who came and built his house next to me. Such a long time ago.

Ripped and Torn

by Georgette Geppert Buckley

When I was young, I only knew of bell bottom jeans. They started out a stiff dark blue and softened and lightened as they wore in. If you accidentally ripped or tore them you ironed on a patch or turned them into cutoffs. Nowadays, you can buy them already ripped, torn, cutoff, cut out, cropped, patched, repaired, destructed, distressed, destroyed or shredded. The hems can be already cuffed, fringed, frayed or raw.

I thought this all was absurd…but then my knee was injured and swollen up after a nasty fall. I missed wearing my jeans. I hobbled into a thrift store and found some soft stretch jeans with one of the tears in the left knee. They were so comfortable but I needed a little more room for that knee. So, I cut out the vertical white shredding and enlarged the rip creating a flap. Then it was just right.

Seven years later, they are still so comfortable. They are perfect to wear in spring, summer and during heat spells. However, lately mosquitos have bitten my exposed knee. I have been thinking of patching the cut out that is a little high in the thigh. I certainly will not turn them into cutoffs at this age.

Maybe I am so comfortable with these jeans because my youthful spirit has been cropped. My soul has been ripped, torn, cut and patched leaving me distressed. I've been acclimating to my new senior life these last four years trying to repair my destructed health. Feeling at times raw, hemmed in, on the fringe, rolled out and frayed. Off the cuff, this year's diagnosis may be the result of Long COVID. And so, the fabric of life continues as my soul mends.

Adrift

by Georgette Geppert Buckley

Tide knocks me
back and forth
to and fro
left and right…

Grey sky meets
grey water
let the tides
come what may.

Does it mean
anything at all?
We are all doomed
to shades of grey.

Tossing and turning
all evening
lost in a sea
of maybe…

The wind blows
the curtains
open and closed
to and fro…

The miniblinds
clang back and forth
let in light and dark
dark and light…

Was I asleep
was it a dream
was it true?
Dream or true…

First Drive

BY GEORGETTE GEPPERT BUCKLEY

One Saturday afternoon as my mom was driving my little sister and I home from grocery shopping and sneaking a visit to Grandma Turner's, I asked if I could drive. Mom replied, "Sure, I wondered when you would ask." She pulled the car over to the side of the unmarked road. Then we switched places. I slowly began to accelerate our family's automatic station wagon. I was excited but nervous as the only car I had never driven was at Disneyland's Autopia where there is a track to keep you in the lane.

I drove the slightly bumpy rock road easily, relieved that since we were in the middle of nowhere, between Nashville and Oakdale, Illinois, no one passed by. To the right, our neighbor's huge weathered barn came into view then their field, edged only by aged wooden poles and barbed wire to keep their cattle in. On the left, was our back field where spring green tuffs of winter wheat my dad and uncle planted.

When I reached the end of the road, I turned the wheel successfully to the left onto the oiled road and proceeded by the red-roofed, white wooden two-story unplumbed house that my older sister and I inhabited. We shared one of four rooms on the bottom floor. Then I turned onto our rock road and stopped in front of our doorless red-roofed two car garage.

In the sunflower yellow kitchen that night at dinner in the adjoining two-bedroom trailer, Mom bragged to Dad that I had driven well for an 8th grader. We happily ate the asparagus that had sprouted magically outside of the large garden we had planted for our 4-H project where Grandpa had helped us measure by pacing his size twelve feet. My older sister had won a blue ribbon for her giant zucchini at the county fair. We also enjoyed our fresh beefsteaks, green beans and potatoes (from the cellar). My favorite was the peach pie that mom baked for dessert. Instead of canning, she had cleverly sliced fresh summer peaches combined with filling, placed them in small plastic containers and stored them in the summer kitchen's upright freezer.

No One Wins in War

BY BRIDGETTE CALLAHAN

"Imagination allows you to bend the rules of the temporal world. I just want them to see that a more beautiful world exists beyond the confines of your environment."

—Amy Sherald, portrait artist

On Sunday, October 1, 2023, my mom and her sister landed at Ben Gurion Airport near Tel Aviv, Israel. For much of the year, they had talked of a trip to Israel, where my half-brother lives. On March 27th, the day they had planned to buy tickets for a summer trip, Ben Gurion was partially closed—all departures were halted—due to striking workers and violent protests of a proposal to limit the Israeli Supreme Court's power. When they heard of the airport's closing, which we had all misunderstood as a complete cessation of flights, they scrapped the summer plans and stopped chatting about visiting the Holy Land.

By mid-summer, their plans had resumed, and they ordered tickets for an early fall trip. I still harbored concern about the Supreme Court issue—Israelis remained divided over the proposed changes—but I had no idea that something would soon happen to unite its people.

After arriving in Israel, my mom and her sister quickly left Karmiel, my brother's city in northern Israel, for a short trip to Jerusalem. On Friday, October 6th, my aunt texted to let me know they were "Back in Karmiel." Along with her message, she sent two happy face emojis sporting sunglasses.

And on Saturday, October 7th, Israel was attacked by Hamas, a Palestinian political and military organization. My aunt reported "that Hamas did a sneak attack early morning on Israel…and Netanyahu has declared war." At first, she didn't realize how serious the conflict was. She didn't know that within a week, she would be heading home with the aid of an American group of veterans called Project DYNAMO. What began as a trip to see my brother and the Holy Land had turned into an emergency, all-expenses paid evacuation from a "war zone," as my aunt put it, to the group's headquarters in Tampa, Florida.

My mom, on the other hand, refused to be evacuated from Israel. She reported just a few days after the conflict began that "I don't have any intention to cut this trip short"—"this is where I am supposed to be!" Later, she said, "I am not ready to leave." (I have to admire her spunky resistance.) In yet another message, she remarked, "Living here [in Israel], people get used to potential problems. God wins! He's in charge."

I imagine that the leaders of Hamas, too, believe that God wins and that He is in charge.

Just the other day, my neighbor—a sage, Middle Eastern man—asked from across the street how my mom was doing. I hesitated, aimed for a you're-not-going-to-believe-this tone, and tried to project my voice across the street: "She's in Israel," I said, throwing up my hands.

At that, he started walking my way, so I crossed the street to speak with him face-to-face. Still standing in the road, I explained how my mom had ended up in Israel, and he mentioned to me that the father of another of our neighbors was in Gaza. I knew the elderly neighbor as the grandfather of a toddler he follows around our cul-de-sac when he visits. I also remembered that the man and his family once gave a bag of lemons and oranges to my mom.

Avoiding an oncoming car, I moved closer to my neighbor as he posed what I interpreted to be a rhetorical question: "What would you do if your land was taken from you?"

My immediate thought? *I wouldn't do what Hamas is doing.* But I kept my conjecture to myself, shrugging my shoulders instead, so he further explained his position on the conflict. He said with frustration that people who are fighting for their land are labeled *terrorists*. My mind went to the various atrocities I'd been hearing about on the news and the fact that I myself had used the word *terrorists* in connection to Hamas.

My neighbor asked, again, "What would *you* do?" My inner-thought was the same: *Well, I wouldn't do what* they're *doing*.

It terrifies me to ask myself, but how can I possibly know what I would or would not do? As I write this, my belief is that I'd sooner kill myself than commit any of the atrocities I've been hearing about. But reeling through my brain, I hear a phrase that one of my sons-in-law, a nurse, used in a conversation we had last night about human nature: *Self-preservation*. I acknowledge that humans can be cruel to each other—that we tend to worry about ourselves more than we worry about our neighbor. But I don't like the idea of self-preservation ruling human beings.

I want to believe in the innate goodness of humans, and I expressed my frustration to my son-in-law: "I. *Don't*. Understand," I said. "why someone would flee the scene of an accident. Don't they know that that would only make things worse? Don't they know that someone could die if they were to leave instead of calling for help?" We talked about the roles of emotion and logic, concluding that people who "hit and run" are acting on emotion and not being rational. *Self-preservation*. We didn't speak of Israel or the Gaza Strip, but I saw the connection.

As I said to my son-in-law, I'd like to think that I would do the right thing if I accidentally hit someone with my car. I'd like to believe that I would *not* run. But I've never been in that situation, so how can I really know what I would do?

Here's what I know: My neighbor's father is in Gaza. My mother is in Israel, where my brother lives.

God wins. They gave my mother a bag of fruit. What would you do…? Self-preservation.

This morning on the CBS news, just over two weeks after the conflict began, Mideast scholar Hussein Ibish delivered impassioned words that are helping me come to terms with my conflicting thoughts: "Nothing can excuse the terrorist rampage by Hamas. They *murdered* hundreds of Israelis and made *no* preparations for the two million people of Gaza to survive the inevitable retaliation. Israel is responsible for avoidable civilian deaths and for cutting off all basic necessities for the Gaza Palestinians now under collective attack."

As Ibish concludes, "Israelis and Palestinians must re-humanize each other.... We are all no better and no worse than each other."

Here's what I know: In war, no one wins.

We Real Small

BY BRIDGETTE CALLAHAN

After Gwendolyn Brooks

The Park Players at Dusk—
Seven with Pails and Shovels:

We pre-school. We
Learn rules. We

Park date. We
Play late. We

Throw dirt. We
Get hurt. We

Cry loud. We
Leave crowd... We

Alone. We
Go home. We

Eat fast. We
Have bath. We

See moon... We
Learn soon.

Dead Flowers

by Ellen Davidson Cantor

faded old jeans lovingly worn
curled arthritic fingers clutching a coffee cup
folded love notes lost in an old volume
falling autumn leaves detaching from trees
scattered seeds on a windy day

Dead Flowers

picked up to grasp anew
photographed to remember
preserved forever
revisited numerous times
holding their fragrance close

capturing
cherished moments

 as flowers fade and die
possibilities arise
for another bloom

 in love there is sadness
in sadness there is hope
through hope, I seek wholeness
keeping us as one
always

Joy

BY ELLEN DAVIDSON CANTOR

the garden dances
with the wind as a partner
and songbirds as melody
twirling, swirling, whirling

surging, twisting, stretching
seeking nourishment
ascending new heights

Yarrow, Pittosporum, Myoporum
Germander, Cranesbill, Mexican Sage

emerge
as shiny gemstones

atop circular shapes
brimming with stones
a Japanese Maple flourishes

Learning to Thrive

by Ellen Davidson Cantor

the trees stand
stark against the blue sky
empty brown sticks
reach toward the heavens
naked
waiting for life to appear

sprawling branches
broken twigs
crunchy leaves,
circular seed balls

all missing

life
spirals forward
retraces its steps
continues the quest
toward a new season

growth is oblique
                                        reaching out
                pulling back

thriving

Memory Fades

by Ellen Davidson Cantor

everywhere there is breakage
life cradles us, cracks, departs without warning

summer flowers disappear into the murky earth
abandoned possessions become rubble
torn and shredded paper deletes our daily tasks
shattered computers capture our information
cracked phones leave us disconnected

illness overtakes the body with tiny spots growing into massive cancer

the earth swallows up loved ones
allowing only visitations in my mind

everywhere there is breakage
life cradles us, cracks, departs without warning

memory fades each time the sun goes down

You Belong Here

BY ELLEN DAVIDSON CANTOR

standing beneath the towering canopy
under massive sycamores reaching skyward
graceful ash trees spread their limbs of shade
eucalyptus embrace the sky
surrounded by a multitude of growth

You belong here

viewing the flourishing grass
abundant from the rain
watering the multitude of pots
overflowing with red geraniums
lovingly cutting hydrangeas

You belong here

planting begonias the color of love
trimming jade trees from another century
coaxing japanese maples in shades of wine
feeding gritty coffee grounds to acid loving plants
nurturing tangy citrus trees

You belong here

worn, tattered garden gloves
saving hands from thorns
lovingly carrying the sweet scent
of pastel roses into vases

You belong here

lush and dense
your sanctuary of ambitious efforts
hummingbirds drinking sugar water
butterflies illuminating the sky
chopping, cutting, weeding

You belong here

your spirit is everywhere
quietly watching over
our garden of joyous memories
reminding me
You are still here

Growing a Garden

A Repetition Poem

BY ALBEN CHAMBERLAIN

If you believe you're ready
to run the nation, give
orders to generals, and choose
the best cabinet officials ever…

Try growing a garden.

If you think you have
the answers to life's problems
so everyone should listen to
all of your wise opinions…

Try planting a garden.

If you believe you've cornered
the market on knowledge and
can explain how everything ought
to work to maximize success…

Try explaining garden soil.

If you think you're ready
to give marching orders to
your wife and children as
emperor of your household kingdom…

Try weeding a garden

If you believe the world
revolves around you and everyone
ought to acknowledge your brilliance
and get out of your way…

Try maintaining a garden.

If you wish to become
the greatest architect and builder
and erect beautiful and monumental
structures that will last forever…

Try building up garden soil.

If you think you can
teach anything to anybody because
of your natural talent and
special gifts inherited at birth…

Try teaching garden birds to sing.

If you believe you have
some new message to deliver
that's never been spoken by
another person in human history…

Try speaking to garden bees.

If you think you're ready
to manage a mega-corporation
with a thousand moving parts
and constantly generate massive profits…

Try managing a garden.

If you believe you understand
the mind of God and can tell
others how they should live
while passing through this world…

Try guiding your garden.

If you think you're ready
to handle fame and adulation
by adoring fans because you
can sing, act, or dance…

Try impressing a garden.

Everyone who gains great knowledge,
power, fame, or achieves financial
success in this wide world
must start close to home.

Try starting in your garden.

Everyone who demonstrates great wisdom,
insight, ability to teach, lead others
or to express valuable opinions
starts their journey at home.

Try starting a garden yourself.

Science Fiction Sestina

BY ALBEN CHAMBERLAIN

In science fiction there's only one plot
since Mary Shelly wrote her *Frankenstein* story.
Scientists go too far and, in their hubris,
create dire situations they can't control.
Then, someone steps in to save
humanity from the scientist's mistake.

It isn't always a monster that results from their mistake.
There are infinite ways for a writer to twist this plot,
when there are people you need to save.
It's part of the never-ending story
where some men seek to control
nature's forces in their hubris.

There are many ways we see this hubris
and there's always a different mistake.
Science seeks to understand and control
nature, resulting in many a turn in plot.
In science fiction there's always a story
to tell and people the hero needs to save.

Sometimes there is a planet to save
from a wiley villain in his hubris.
There's always a way to build a story,
once you understand the big mistake.
There are many twists and turns to plot
since it's the writer who has control.

Every story eventually comes down to control
since the villain has no desire to save,
but always manipulates people in his plot.

It always ends when his hubris
leads him to some big mistake
and his downfall to end the story.

So even though it's a generic story,
the writer must exercise his control.
Don't ever make the mistake
thinking there's nothing new to say or save.
Even writers get tripped by their hubris
when they fail to take charge of the plot.

So go, find yourself a story to tell and some people for you to save.
As the author, take control and don't succumb to the snare of hubris
It's never a mistake to create a new turn in the old generic plot.

On Climate Change

A Duplex Poem

BY ALBEN CHAMBERLAIN

Climate change to our earth is all around,
in the atmosphere, the oceans, and on the ground.

We see changes in the atmosphere, oceans, and ground,
because our human "wisdom" can't be found.

Our human "wisdom" will never be found
as long as our greed and "needs" abound.

As long as our human greed and "needs" abound
we'll keep driving our fragile environments down.

Humans will keep driving our fragile environments down
until the breaking point finally comes around.

When the breaking point finally comes around,
no place of sanctuary for our species will be found.

No place of sanctuary for our species will be found,
because climate change to our earth is all around.

Grandma Vibes

BY NATALIE CHAMPION

Kieran

Lover of books, trains, excavators, fire trucks, and ambulances,

Marathon runner at the tender age of two,

Chasing after Kieran at the Zoo Safari Park,

Losing the stroller,

Natasha says, "Mama, you left the stroller!"

I say, "But I caught up with Kieran!"

I see me in Kieran

I see Natasha in Kieran

But Kieran is the bravest

Riding a mare called Wendy for his second birthday,

Devouring melty cheese pizza and vanilla cake with creamy
    turquoise frosting

Surrounded by family

Enveloped in their warm embraces

But grandma's hug is the best

Counting the days until the next visit…

Being a grandma is the best!

Love you always Kieran!

Love,

Grandma

Ode to Grandma Rita

by Natalie Champion

Chatting with grandma

Remembering her funny grandma jokes

Her smiling face at my wedding

The violin player serenading her

Remembering her visits full of joy and love

Especially the Disneyland trip where I was so sleepy, I put my
underwear on backwards

And grandma laughed heartily

Fearlessly riding the Matterhorn past the yeti and zooming
down the mountain

Roaring through Big Thunder Mountain on a runaway train

And a wild ride on Space Mountain

Her boundless energy and joy

Playing Scrabble and grandma always won

Her mind forever sharp

Grandma was my cheerleader

Cheering me on when I played the Wicked Witch of the West
in my senior high school play

Now her 102-year-old mind wanders,

Never stopping

Her strength flows in my veins

Love you always grandma!

Your beloved granddaughter,

Natalie

Quixotic

BY RICK CHAMPION

Sancho insisted. "Sire, those are windmills, of which we have many in La Mancha. You well know that the peasant plows and sows; seeds sprout with the warmth of the sun; harvest comes; the miller grinds and the cook bakes. Then we eat."

Don Quixote had a different view. "The untrained eye sees a windmill. The warrior recognizes a ferocious giant, in disguise, upon yonder hill. And there is not just one giant, but many, one for each peak."

"Note, Friend, that these giants have four arms rather than the usual two, thus doing greater damage."

Sancho's impatience was growing. "Sire, what you perceive as arms are the vanes of the windmill, which, gathering force from the wind, turn the gears, and so grind the grain into flour.

Rocinante snorted, "Friend mule, I see two fools."

"There is but one fool," replied the mule, "Don Quixote, who mistakes the windmill for a giant."

Rocinante corrected the mule. "One fool fails to understand a common agricultural machine. The other fool lacks judgment. He believes that Don Quixote can be ruled by reason but he is, in fact, captured by delusion."

The Knight urgently demanded, "Friend Sancho, strap on to me my buckler, helmet, and gauntlet. Arm me with spear and mace. Prepare Rocinante for battle. Arm yourself. Forget not to protect your beast with steel."

Sancho asked, "Why this harebrained fantasy of doing battle with giants?"

Don Quixote answered, "Would you want a troop of giants to conquer our homeland of La Mancha? Recall that Toboso, the abode of my Lady Dulcinea, is nearby. Might not a ferocious giant breach the walls of her town to carry her away as a lovely captive? I am sworn to defend her!

The giants may have fearful hair and beard, hungry mouths, and burning eyes, but be not cowardly! Attack!"

Rocinante reared on her hind legs saying, "I am hungry, tired, thirsty, and on the edge of sunstroke, "As the famous Spanish dramatist Federico García Lorca, writes in *La casa de Bernarda Alba*, the sun falls like hot lead." Rocinante neighed with disgust.

The mule was mystified. "Hot lead? Are you literate?"

"Ass," replied Rocinante. "Just because I can read is no reason for you to be jealous."

"You insult me," said the mule. "That line is from the twentieth century. We are in the sixteenth."

Their bickering was cut short when the Knight shouted, "Charge!"

As the attack began, the giants flailed their arms. The wind began to stir.

The mule complained, "I'm tired of running with the one of excessive girth on my back. And I rejoined Rocinante, tired of the skinny one who insists on wearing steel.

The same thought occurred to both animals. On the count of three Sancho and the Knight crashed to earth with the clang of steel.

The mule asked, "Should we leave them?" Rocinante considered. "Such bravery, even though foolish, merits loyalty. We stay."

The mule sniffed. "I smell water and fresh grass. We graze until they recover."

Don Quixote ached, "Friend Sancho, I see stars. Next time, we bring a regiment."

Rocinante was certain that there would be no next time.

Don't Ask for a Rubber

BY SYLVIA CLARKE

"We have to check the accounts again," Mr. Bohner announces. "We are still off by…", and he names an amount. Red pencil in hand, I prepare to add a red dot in front of the black pen and pencil dots already by each figure in the ledger. It's the summer between my junior and senior years at Cedar Lake Academy, the secondary boarding school I attend, and I have been working in the school's business office since before school started last fall.

When I first arrived a year earlier, I wondered how someone I didn't know could greet me by name during our first meeting. Now I know: she worked in the business office and saw the names of students as their initial payments came in for school fees. Now I was one who could surprise students by calling them by name before they knew mine.

Working in that office I learn more about bookkeeping than I had in the class taken earlier, including the importance of accuracy. Sometimes I check adding machine tapes multiple times before I find the lost penny when I balance out the cash drawer at the end of the day. Usually, when the deficit is nine cents or a multiple of it, the problem is a pair of transposed numbers—for example, 31 vs 13. Do I have number dyslexia?

I enjoy the variety of tasks—becoming proficient on the adding machine; helping prepare student statements to be sent to parents; stuffing envelopes; keeping inventory of the pens, paper, books, and other items sold through a small back office store window. While working in that room, I can hear exchanges between those coming to purchase an extra pencil or notepad as they chat with the student presiding at the window.

Imagine the consternation of the sales person when a student who grew up in another country comes to ask for a rubber. How is he or she to know that in English used outside the USA, that is what an eraser is called? Worse yet is the embarrassment of the purchaser after finding out the true meaning of the word in this country. Guess I could say I also learned "Don't ask for a rubber" —unless I know what the word means where I am.

Dream

by Sylvia Clarke

I'm holding a naked baby when she starts fidgeting. I recognize she is about to urinate so grab some cloth to put under her to catch it. As I wake from this dream, the color yellow comes to mind and a question: *"How did I know the wiggling was a signal she was going to wet?"*

Go back with me to the late 1960s. Wil and I are in Tanzania where he teaches math and some science at a secondary boarding school. I am reaching out to people who live near the school by organizing story and visual materials for groups of students who go out on weekends to conduct Bible story hours with children in nearby villages. Mrs. King, a fellow missionary, brought a medium-sized accordion with her from the U.S. but doesn't know how to play it. She loans it to me, and I carry it up the hill with one group of students and accompany the songs they teach the children who gather in a small thatch roofed shed.

One week I learn that a woman in one of the neighboring families has an infected wound on her foot. I know how water treatments can help such problems, so I visit her *kijiji*–village–and try to help by soaking the sore foot in heated water. Afterwards, as I sit on the ground with the women and visit, I admire the baby one young mother is holding, so she hands me her baby. I note her smooth skin and the tiny curls on her head. Baby seems content for a while but then begins to squirm. That's when I decide to hold her differently and lift her up over my lap. Before I can react, baby lets fly, and the women all laugh. My skirt's now wet.

I always wondered how these African mothers keep their un-diapered babies from getting them and their carrying clothes dirty. Now I begin to realize: the babies let them know they need to go! And unlike me, these mothers recognize the signals.

Oh, and I am wearing one of my favorite outfits—a matching yellow blouse and skirt set.

Elephants

by Sylvia Clarke

There they come, huge gray unmistakable shapes moving behind a screen of small trees and brush. L.T., our driver and guide, spots them and stops the vehicle to allow us to watch them leisurely stroll not fifty feet away. Soon my gaze fastens on the smallest one as it ambles from one bunch of grass to another, twisting its tiny trunk around dried stems and stuffing them in its mouth. How darling!

I draw in my breath as this small one turns from the flank of the parade and heads purposefully toward us on the dirt track where we sit in the open back of the safari vehicle. Does it think it can scare us away? The thought soon passes as I watch it plant itself next to a patch of grass and begin to break off pieces to munch on. Oh, I realize, it just sees more food!

Purpose and persistence mark its movements as this young elephant calf also tugs at small bits of shrub. I can tell this is serious eating time. Others in the herd also focus on edibles, so, I conclude, this little one is learning to do the same. As my companions capture multiple pictures, I am completely enamored until L.T. starts the motor, and we move on. These are the first elephants we have seen, so I wonder, "Will we see more?"

The answer is "Yes!" In fact, we learn that Botswana's Chobe National Park is known for its large elephant population and see evidence of that as we catch glimpses of other elephant families through the bush or along the river. Some even stand out among the herds of tan impala on the large green island we see near the river shore during our bumpy ride. This kind of ride is giving us what L.T. calls an "African massage."

Meanwhile we come upon young kudu males practicing their moves to gain dominance, more and more impala with their black ankles and backside parentheses, usually browsing peacefully together, and even a pair of neck banging teen giraffes. Later in the day, during a boat ride on Chobe River, we come upon a larger elephant herd starting to cross the river. This group includes small ones, too. L.T. maneuvers our boat near others lined up to allow passengers to watch the crossing from a safe distance.

I watch as the matriarch steps in followed by several other adults. "How deep is the river here?" I wonder. Soon they are tailed by two little ones that stay close on their heels. I cannot tell whether they hold onto a tail in front of them but do see their trunks snorkel above the water as do those of other calves until the whole herd safely reaches the Zambian shore. I am still in awe of how God made such huge creatures with all the right parts to navigate their world and survive.

Mom Esther

BY SYLVIA CLARKE

It's 1971, and our family is visiting my in-laws in Africa on the way to the USA where Wil intends to work on his PhD. Esther, my mother-in-law, calls. "Come, Sylvia, rest your hands and face." She leads the way into the living room and sits in an easy chair across from the couch where I plop down, glad for a break. Keeping up with our active two-and-a-half-year-old daughter at Ouma and Oupa's house is not a relaxing occupation. Somehow Mom Esther knows just what I need, thus this invitation to rest.

My relationship with Esther Clarke began even before Wilton and I were even engaged. Knowing she would soon be finished with the coursework for her Master's degree and heading back to Africa, Esther wanted to become acquainted with the girl her son was dating. She and Dad Clarke not only visited me one weekend at my parent's home in Adrian, Michigan, but also came to the college Wil and I both attended and ate with us in the cafeteria at least once.

It was there I noticed she kept looking for encouraging signs that I might be a good wife for her older son. I guess I overheard a comment she made to Dad when I shared a cherry from my fruit salad with Wil. That made me realize how hard she was looking for all the good she could find. I began to recognize her as someone focused on the positive.

When summer came, Esther and Fred, Wilton's father, invited me to join them and Wil on their trip to say goodbye to relatives and friends before heading to the ship that would return them to their work in Africa. I've forgotten how I traveled to their apartment in East Lansing but remember being welcomed by Esther's hug and Fred's twinkling eyes. While Esther finished her final exams, she encouraged Wil and me to rent a canoe and spend an hour or so paddling on the Grand River that ran through the

Michigan State University campus. The next day I headed north with the Clarkes to visit their relatives in the Traverse City area.

There I first met Dad's two sisters, Flora and Mildred, and some of Wilton's cousins. We stayed with Flora and her husband Martin who seemed to rub Mom Esther entirely the wrong way. What stands out in my mind, however, is Esther's response to Fred the morning we were leaving for the next leg of the journey when he kept urging, "Let's go," or "Hurry up!"

"Now Fred," Esther finally replied, "I'm getting ready and will be there soon, so please don't rush me!"

"Wow," I thought. "She's not just a pushover. She can stand up for herself!" It was a lesson I needed because I always seemed to be trying to please everyone else, a frustrating and unhealthy process.

Mom Esther was a superb storyteller, and when we slept in the same room while visiting her cousin Marion near Chicago, Illinois, I remember she told me the story of toddler Wilton and the enema can. This was a metal container coated with enamel that Wilton had somehow damaged so that the metal could rust. "I scolded him soundly," she confessed. "I should never have done that. The can kept working just fine after that."

I understood Mom's point. She was teaching me to pick my battles when I had children and overlook the small, unimportant matters. Quite an educator, Mom Esther.

Eight years later, she is still educating—this time by example when she calls, "Come, Sylvia, rest your hands and face" in her home at Solusi College in Rhodesia—now Zimbabwe. Mom Esther's lesson has stayed with me through the years and still blesses me today.

My Afterlife

BY WIL CLARKE

I'm eighty-two years old and the afterlife is rushing up on me, with a vengeance. What do I think will happen to me when it actually catches me? Here are several scenarios, arranged in the reverse order of what I consider to be their probabilities.

1. *Reincarnation*: In this scenario, since I have not lived a perfect life I will return to do my life over again. I have, jokingly, told people that I will not be a mathematician again—too many people hate the very ground I walk on!

2. *Eternal Joy or Torture*: A popular Christian scenario. This requires a god who by one means or another has been keeping track of my doings. If I have achieved sufficient credit I will experience a life of bliss forever and ever. On the other hand if I don't have sufficient credit, I will suffer eternal torment. In either case this god must be a tyrant of the most heinous form. How can any being live with him/her self if they are aware of beings in unending torture? Or how can they award bad people like Adolf Hitler or Idi Amin eternal joy without payment for all the pain they have inflicted on their fellow humans? In either case I would rather not know such a god.

3. *Annihilation*: The only possible scientific scenario. In this case once I die, all life functions cease. My molecules disintegrate. According to philosopher-scientists like Carl Sagan, I am made of star-stuff and this star-stuff lies around forever or until some of it is used to form other life forms, which in turn face annihilation.

4. *Christian Heaven/Hell*: I will be in heaven or hell. If I am perfect I will continue on in a new existence, where pain and sorrow, evil and strife cannot exist. If I am not perfect my every attribute, body and soul, will be forever destroyed

in the "purifying" fires of hell—I will be annihilated. There is a third scenario, since no person is perfect, or can be perfect, Jesus Christ suffered hell for me. His grace gives me the reward of the perfect, purely because I have accepted this reward that I didn't earn. This grace is equally available to everyone.

As the philosopher/mathematician Blaise Pascal (1623-1662) reasoned, there are exactly four choices open to a person:

- If God does not exist and I do not believe in Him I face annihilation.

- If God does not exist and I do believe in Him I face annihilation, with possible loss of some sacrifices made in vain.

- If God does exist and I do not believe in Him I face annihilation and infinite loss.

- If God does exist and I do believe in Him, I face some possible loss of some sacrifices I made, but with immeasurable and infinite gain.

He, of course, concluded that the only wise choice of action is to believe in God. My choice coincides with Pascal's.

Paris, January 19, 1976

BY WIL CLARKE

We had been called to go to Africa as missionaries. I had just finished earning my doctorate in Mathematics from the University of Iowa, and we had spent Christmas with Sylvia's parents in Michigan. We were awaiting a visa to enter South Africa. I spent my days shoveling the new snow that seemed to be a daily occurrence and chafing at the bit to get to work. My parents were missionaries in Rhodesia, Africa. They were eagerly awaiting us.

I phoned the secretary of the mission board: "If you get us to Salisbury in Rhodesia, which doesn't require a visa for Americans, I'll get us into South Africa." I knew how to do it!

"Okay?!" The secretary sounded incredulous. We finally got tickets to Salisbury, Rhodesia (now Harare, Zimbabwe.)

In the early morning, our red-eye special landed at Charles de Gaulle International Airport northeast of Paris. The airport officials were very solicitous of our welfare. They placed us on a chartered bus to take us to Orly International Airport south of Paris. When the airline representatives met us, they told us they had a special day room for us to await our flight that evening.

Sylvia showed her late pregnancy. I got her, Esther, 6, and Julia, 3, settled in the room. She was going to take a warm bath and relax. We put the girls to bed, since none of us had had much sleep on the plane.

"I'm going to go down and get our boarding passes. Please don't come there because they will see you and may give us trouble on account of your condition."

The line was long at the South African Airways counter. I waited there as the line slowly moved. Finally, after well over a half an hour, I was just stepping up to the window when Sylvia waddled up looking very pregnant.

The window was manned by South Africans who didn't have the grace of the Parisians who had been so gracious to us. "Is she going with you on this plane?" the woman behind the window demanded.

"Yes, she is; here's her ticket."

"No she's not!" she stated.

Then proceeded a long interchange of "Yes she is!" "No! she isn't!"

Meanwhile the line continued to grow longer and longer and impatience was growing.

"Wait a minute!" she demanded, and disappeared into the back room.

Meanwhile I was praying earnestly.

A tall man came out from the back. Looking me squarely in the eye he almost shouted in a strong South African accent: "In no ways am I going to let her on my plane!"

I was stunned. What was I going to do in this strange city with only $300 in my pocket, and a very pregnant wife and two kids?

"All right," I spoke with equal authority. "I have our tickets for the plane. I have bookings for this plane. I have a letter from my wife's doctor okaying this trip. You are stopping us. Therefore, you will pay for a place for us to stay here in Paris. You will pay for all hospital expenses for the baby to be born. You will pay all of our expenses until it is time for us to fly on to Cape Town."

I was bluffing. Surely, he knew it! It was only a direct answer to my prayer that made me say what I did and then drove it home into his unwilling mind. He came from a country where they were used to constantly mistreating their subjects.

He looked totally stunned. He stood there uncertainly for a bit. Suddenly he said, "Wait here!" As though I were going to run away. He disappeared and came back with a hand full of forms. "Sign here!" he pointed. "And here," and he pointed again, until I had signed a bunch of release forms. Then he handed us our boarding passes.

Sylvia had stood there dumbfounded the whole time. I turned to her, "Hi hon' what were you going to ask me?" To this day, she has not remembered what it was!

Poison Ivy/Poison Oak

BY WIL CLARKE

Our family was touring the United States in 1956. We stopped to visit Dad's Uncle Meade and Aunt Minnie MacGuire in Sonora, California. My brother, Elwood, was 11 and I was 14. We loved running around in short pants and barefoot through the grass and trees near their home. Scattered through the tall grass were lots of poison oak plants, which we were unfamiliar with because they don't grow in Africa where we grew up. After each day, Mom would dutifully grab our clothes, throw them over her arm and take them down stairs and wash them.

Within a couple days Mom's arms began to itch and then break out into a rash that oozed puss. She tried using calamine lotion, but it had very little effect. For at least a fortnight, she was in torture as we drove through the hot summer air in a VW Microbus with no air conditioning. Elwood and I seemed to be totally unaffected by the devil's vine.

Seventeen years later, I was studying in Iowa City and got permission to grow a vegetable garden in a newly acquired vacant lot. After a farmer came in and plowed the lot, my family and some friends descended on the lot and weeded the area, pulling much of the stuff out by its roots. Since it was early spring and it had been so recently plowed there were no leaves to identify most of the weeds. Two or three days later, my hands and arms started to itch, one of my eyes swelled shut and itched so badly I wanted to tear it out of its socket. I finally gave up and went in to see the doctor at the student health office at the University of Iowa. He took one look at me and said bluntly, "Do you have it on your genitals?"

Blushing wildly, and not being used to talking openly about my nether parts, I stuttered and mumbled.

"You've got poison ivy!" he informed me.

"It can't be, I'm not allergic to it." And I told him of Mom's experience.

"I don't care—it's poison ivy. I'll give you an antihistamine/steroid shot and it will dry it up." It dried it up within a few short hours—but the itch lasted the usual fortnight.

We had a beautiful, sporty red and black Ford Torino that I loved to drive. It would purr along at 120 miles per hour without hardly trying. Sylvia and I harnessed our two girls in the back seat, this was before kids' car seats became generally available. We headed across the roasting western deserts without air conditioning to visit family in California.

I experienced Mom's discomfort, and was finally able to commiserate with her. Had she been around, I'm sure she would have laughed and said, "It serves you right!" This was but the beginning of my decades' long, fierce battle with the poison ivy/oak. Thank goodness there's none on these local hills in Riverside. But there is plenty in all the mountains around us—beware!

In my battle with poison ivy/oak I found the Indian remedy: bathe the affected area with cold tea produced by boiling the whole plant of Jewelweed or Touch-Me-Not. Do this continuously for several hours. This works well in the eastern part of the country where jewelweed grows naturally near where poison ivy is found. Remember the old words of counsel: "Leaves of three—Let them be!"

A homeopathic remedy, Rhus Tox, works well especially if taken orally before coming in contact with the poison. And a prescription steroid cream, Triamcinolone, works well when applied directly to the lesions. However, never consider giving up walking and hiking in the great outdoors, the health benefits far outweigh the annoyances.

Astronomers Want to Be Astronauts Too

BY JAMES COATS

Even in the darkness
I know my way across
the infinity of you.

I have mapped out goosebumps
each by name like constellations
along your heavenly body.

Caught up in the gravity of weightier ideas
you pull me into onyx transcendence
light swallowed in the blackness of pupils.

Call me adventure, seeking out life
or life seeking out another life
where others thought none existed.

I wished to revolve around a space
that was not me, until your reflection
mirrored all that ever was.

From stardust we were made
and with star magic I return
A distant traveler finding home in you.

Like an ever expanding connection
we are tethered to our conception,
let the Galaxy echo us in praise.

Deep space exploration has never
felt this intimate, this quantum entanglement
of matter making eternity matter.

Take me in, prism me like the visual spectrum
as I supernova across your universe
only to be reborn a star on your lips.

Swallow my light
and deliver me to the black
back to the womb of beginning.

Where beauty was belonging
or a comet
in the eye of a forgotten nebula.

For as rare a jewel as earth may be
I would be nothing, if not for your atmosphere
that gives my lungs breath.

I Might Be a Supervillain

by Elinor Cohen

"If you've never taken one of my classes before, you should know that I like to start off with an icebreaker," said the man on Zoom with the most excruciatingly perfect mustache I had ever seen during all my years and all my travels on Earth. A mustache so exquisite that you would remember it if you saw it many years later in a photograph. Far more involved than a classic curly Imperial Handlebar, thicker than a silly Salvador Dalí, less upside-down horseshoe than a Hulk Hogan. Those trendy hipster manicured beard product subscription services were made for this guy. He's probably entered facial hair contests. He's probably won.

I'd enrolled in a series of caregiver classes online, since the general health and well-being of my 83 year old mother was so unpredictable that she was being diagnosed with new diseases just as they were being discovered. These caregiver classes explored everything from taking vital signs and performing CPR to leveraging community resources and understanding basic human needs. I had dozens of pages of handwritten notes on Alzheimer's and Heart Disease and Traumatic Brain Injuries and how to maybe prevent them from happening. My mother, who the caregiver classes referred to as my 'consumer' (capitalist much?), eagerly awaited new information after each 90 minute class, listening carefully as I explained, only to forget most of it almost immediately.

I learned about Psychotic Disorders Including Schizophrenia from the Irish theater major who performed the class like a Disney princess in a serious off-Broadway production. I learned about Blood Borne Pathogens from the retired rabbi who spent his free time hiking the wilderness with his pack of dogs, all of them named after characters from *Star Trek* and one of whom "barks at ghosts" during class sometimes. I learned Fire Safety and Fall Prevention from the optimistic Santa who was the exact stereotype of every naive well-meaning social worker character in every movie ever made. I learned Stress Management and Mindfulness from the visually impaired woman with the relaxing voice who led a guided meditation so satisfying, I wrote a letter to her boss suggesting that she record a YouTube video. But I'd taken four classes with Meticulous Mustache Man, including Emergency and Disaster Preparedness, and he was quickly becoming my favorite. Now he was ready with his icebreaker:

"If you could have one superpower, what would it be?"

Mustache usually kept it light: What's your favorite breakfast food? Do you prefer sweet or savory? Where's your dream vacation location? If you could come back as an animal, which one? and so on. Choosing a superpower seemed like it required minimal effort, because obviously it would be Read Minds or Be Invisible or Fly or something likely to result in personal gain. I thought about a weird movie I stumbled across while browsing the Amazon Prime Video account of someone whose password I used to know, in which former People Magazine's Sexiest Man Alive Idris Elba told a story about genie wishes gone terribly wrong. One wish that seemed to go okay was when the medieval princess wished to Know Every Thing That Is True and Good, pretty cool right? 10 out of 10, would wish it again. Of course she fucked it up one wish later when she decided to forget they ever met.

Anyway, I wrote Know Everything in the chat box of the Zoom call about caregiving in response to Mustache's inquiry. Fly was the most popular answer, with Super Strength and Time Travel and Be Invisible and Live Forever rounding out the top five (no sign of X-Ray Vision anywhere, I guess because you can see almost anyone naked on the internet these days). One lady wrote Eat Whatever I Want And Not Gain A Pound, and that lady probably regretted writing that when she didn't get the Laughing Face emoji that she was no doubt expecting. I typed Know Everything with the kind of arrogant confidence of someone who resisted the self-indulgent urge to say Read Minds In Order To Know Your Darkest Secret And Use It Against You and/or Go On A Game Show And Win Lots Of Money By Already Knowing All The Answers.

I'm so clever. My brain patted itself on the back.

Then Millie with the short hair typed this: Knowing What People Need And Being Able To Give It To Them. I read it again, slower. The thumbs up and heart emojis started rolling in. I read it again, out loud. I felt like my eyes were melting into the back of my head. Knowing What People Need And Being Able To Give It To Them. Who was this person who was so specific about the good she wanted to do in the world? She wanted to save people, heal people, and was this the single most not selfish thing I've ever heard? I wanted to type "I'd like to change my answer to what she said" but I was too embarrassed. Who did I think I was, some ridiculous philosophy major burnout who was taking caregiver classes on Checking Blood Sugar and Injecting Insulin because it's what Aristotle would have done?

Time to face the truth, I'm a Supervillain. An out-of-touch, self-obsessed, slightly condescending, opposite of a superhero, Supervillain. Did I feel bad about it? I think I did.

I spent the rest of the class so distracted; were we learning how to change a colostomy bag? Insert a suppository? I knew there would be a test at the end so I tried to focus and feel less like a bastard. Mustache didn't make a fuss about it when he read the chat message aloud sandwiched in with all the others. He didn't share the profound and inspired and also odd reaction that fell over me.

I had another class with Mustache three weeks later. "If you've ever taken one of my classes before, you know that I like to start off with an icebreaker question. Write your answers in the chat box." And then he said:

"If you put icing on a brownie, does that make it cake?"

Of course it does. But how best to answer? Is this a majority yes or a majority no situation? How do these caregivers feel about cake? I flirted with the idea of writing something cerebral about the metaphor that dessert represents, but quickly talked myself out of it. Still, I wanted to contribute something, so... If you put icing on a brownie, does that make it cake? I typed "Absolutely yes, just like putting frosting on a muffin makes it a cupcake."

Everyone else said no.

Outcast.

Supervillain.

I Want Those Firsts

by Chuck Doolittle

I want to deliver the newspaper to my customers once more,
Tossing all 86 of them right up to the front door
And even mow some of their lawns, like I did so long ago
Loving every minute and making extra dough.

And I crave the chance to relive driving for the very first time,
Obtaining my license in that '56 wagon which was oh, so sublime.
But more than that, I want the chance, to buy my first car again
And cruise around with my girlfriend in tow way back when.

I want a chance to do high school again, and make choices I
    didn't make then.
Choices that would send me on a path to success instead of a
    slight tail spin.
And, oh, would I want to play tennis again on that team that was
    just such a blast.
My coach, teammates, competition, and all, certainly too good to last.

But the jobs, yes, the jobs of my youth, from short-order cooking
    to pumping the gas,
Box boy, stocker, and checker to boot. How I want to be able to
    take one more pass.
All were so fun and left indelible impressions, though none could
    compare to the privilege of teaching.
Shaping young minds, watching them learn, passing on lessons
    hopefully far-reaching.

I want to, again, hold my child for the first time and fly to Russia
    to get her.
And watch the eyes of her mom light up, becoming an instant
    cuddler.
And give her hand away in marriage some twenty-odd years later,
Seeing her grow into a successful woman, a special ed advocator.

Yes, what I desperately want is to revisit those moments in life.
Like the unforgettable first time I laid eyes on my beautiful wife.
To recapture all those "firsts" that are so meaningful to me,
Revisiting what I now hold dear, every sweet memory.

The Chauffeur – A Sonnet

by Chuck Doolittle

She defied the wind, friction had no impact
Hurling her mass at nothing in particular
The beauty and elegance harmoniously intact
Admirers regaled, causing quite the stir
Rivals? Not many, so few could compete
Reasonable given the credentials
Superior quality, mechanically elite
Fully equipped with the essentials
Comparisons were futile, barely coming close
To the experience and mood she could induce
She'd order up the moon and deliver with the most
Breathtaking sensation one could produce.
Fond memories of hanging out and having a bang
Cruising in my chauffeur, my Fastback Ford Mustang.

Thankful

by Chuck Doolittle

The leaves have turned as warm days give way to crisp, cool evenings. It's the beginning of fall in Southern California. The anticipation of the season is in the air, eagerly leaving behind the dog days of summer, replaced by refreshing breezes and morning dew. Short days hint at the promise of Thanksgiving, both heartfelt and celebrated, thankful for gatherings past and future. Friends and loved ones who have passed overtake the forefront of our minds. The anticipation arrives of reminiscing anew, keenly aware of each celebration's ever-fleeting nature. The thankfulness surrounding the annual holiday tradition spills over into our gratitude for time spent with loved ones. One such relationship of mine is most worthy of contemplation.

I held my older brother, Steve, on a pedestal most of my life. In my mind, he was smarter, handier, more popular, and more talented. I envied his ability to take things apart, decipher a problem, and backwards map them together again. I admired his ability to play an instrument, which I never did. He also drove the coolest cars, from sports cars to muscle cars, even a motorcycle, and repaired them himself. He was in marching band and jazz band, and I attended many of his competitions. He was president of the Key Club in high school. Most of all, I admired his tenaciousness. When he went after something, he went all in. When we worked at Safeway together, he became management. He even accomplished something I had wanted to when he became a radio host of a small station in Lake Arrowhead. Despite my feeling slightly inferior at times, I idolized him.

But then it changed. Get-togethers diminished, except for maybe on holidays. One-on-one time ended. Talks on the phone dwindled, eventually ending altogether. Although we had our differences, we'd always found a way to overcome them and remain close. But this time was different. Days and months turned into years, and soon, my only brother and I, though living only 30 miles from each other, were now emotionally miles apart. This distance ate at me year in and year out. Reuniting seemed hopeless. I wasn't sure how my brother viewed this time in our lives, but for me it created an irreplaceable void. The one who would be there when needed for advice, a laugh, walks down memory lane, tech solutions, and to look up to, was out of my life. What's a little brother's identity without a big brother?

But hope began to appear. I began to reach out, relentlessly, refusing to give up, eventually rekindling the flame. And slowly, little by little, over considerable time, a spark began to flicker through the fractures that had formed. And reconciliation finally began through mutual efforts to leave the past behind and move forward.

Today, my brother and I are closer than ever. We took a road trip last year and would like to do another. We get together to hangout and talk over lunch. We text often, menial things, memes, sometimes not about much of anything, which to me is a sign of our renewed closeness. When I told him I was writing a story about him, he replied, "Oh, Lord!" We now are available whenever needed to offer support to one another. We have each other's backs. This Thanksgiving I have much to be thankful for: the gift of life, a loving wife, daughter, and son-in-law, mother, and sister. I have some great friends, an amazing writing class, I don't want for much, and I couldn't be more thankful for the relationship with my big brother.

A Retirement Party for the Ages

BY CHUCK DOOLITTLE

Trying to capture a 30-year career into a single three-hour event is much how I felt at my retirement party. Talk about déjà vu. Thirty years, four different schools, and seeing many of the colleagues from those years will do that.

Walking in with me was a fellow teacher, the woman I met in 1991 at my first teaching assignment. The same woman I married and shared my teaching career with every step of the way, throughout the highs of relationships with students and colleagues, to the lows of pink slips and layoffs, she's been my teaching and life partner in one.

I then glance and see another woman across the patio. Wow! I haven't seen her in 20 years. She was the attendance clerk at my very first school. She always had a smile, a joke, and helped keep the stress of being a new teacher at an even keel. She loved hanging out with all the teacher nerds every chance she got. And she never made you feel like a loser when you made those paperwork errors, which were inevitable for probationary teachers. She had the gift of making a new teacher feel at home.

Sitting by her was the woman, who, along with her husband and three children, would become some of our best friends. We vacationed with them and, when their oldest daughter was born with a heart problem, were there for the two surgeries that followed. They were there when we brought our adopted daughter home from Russia. Their oldest and our daughter would become best friends, right up to this day when both are now newlyweds.

A table away sat my former principal and assistant principal from my final assignment. They were by far the best administrative tandem I've ever worked with in education. They were there when I had my massive heart attack in 2018, unbelievably supportive as I dealt with recovery, fear, and ultimately returning to work. They were also the ones sitting in the room with my grade level team, planning lessons, as we were informed by the superintendent that the COVID-19 outbreak demanded that we be sent home from school, that dark Friday the 13th of March 2020, traversing the chaos with grace, understanding, and utter consideration for all we were going through. I'll never forget their support. I'll never forget them!

Also at their table were three men who would have a profound influence on my life and me. We became close friends whom I felt safe enough to pray with, confide in, and even to hit a driver in front of from the tee. We've lunched together, played together, cried together, and retired together. Better men are hard to find.

Flashes of my long tenure in teaching flooded my mind that June day of 2021. As I looked out across the nostalgia-filled chairs, I saw each person who played a part in my story, enhancing the joy and satisfaction accumulated throughout my career.

A quote found on one of the cards I received that day succinctly summarized my feelings. It read, "The difference between a workplace and a nice place to work is the good people who make it so."

So how do you capture a 30-year teaching career into a single moment? One memory at a time.

Me

by Reiss DuPlessis

I walked through the open door not knowing where it leads.
I only know I should go, I must go.
Who is on the other side of the door waiting for me?
Surprise! It's me, the me I never knew
The me I see awaiting for me to know.
The me I need to know.
But, do I really want to know?
I think, no, I know I want to know
I think I'll like the me who awaits me there.
That me who was willing to wait for me to get there,
The patient me I never was but wanted to be.
Age. Age is the answer. This old me is the me I've been waiting
    to know.
Patient, relaxed and free. Free to be me….this old man I've
    come to be.

The Easement

BY REISS DuPLESSIS

Mrs. Knight's house in Echo Park, built in 1921 and for which she paid sixteen thousand dollars in the nineteen seventies, the house she predicted would, one day, be worth a million dollars, sold in 1922 for two and a quarter million dollars. It was the house she loved with reverence reserved for places of worship or national monuments. It, however, had a couple of issues. The front entrance was a hundred step climb up a hill. The street level entrance was through a long, narrow easement that belonged to the adjacent property and could, legally, be closed by the owner after a government set time frame. The expiration date was close, very close. Those might have been deterrents for other buyers, for her, though, they were challenges and nothing excited her more than a challenge. Nothing would stop her and, weeks before the easement's term limit expiration, the house was hers. The easement had to be available to her. The owner of the easement, Mr. Armstrong, had planned as soon possible, to seal the easement, making the house virtually inaccessible and buy it for a fraction of its current value thereby doubling the size of his property and command of the hill. He did not welcome her and her husband with warmth and neighborly charm. His frustration and anger were not hidden and his dislike for that "pushy woman" was immediate. He'd found, he thought, an easy foe… a bigmouthed redheaded woman. Unlike her gentle, agreeable husband, Mrs. Knight was known for and prideful of her lack of fear, inability to be intimidated and her willingness to take on all comers. The Echo Park war had begun.

The easement was too narrow for most cars and it was the only access to her oddly placed garage. Mrs. Knight had to park on the street and walk down the easement to the back entrance of her house. After sunset, it was dark and threatening. Her first order of business was a timer controlled spotlight that lit the length and width of the long path. Minutes after the light's debut, Mr. Armstrong was knocking at her back door. "Are you crazy? Putting that ridiculous light out there."

"Crazy?" Her responding tone was soft, gentle and sweet. "Dear man, if you want to see crazy, I'll show you crazy!" Her voice, suddenly, thunderous, "now, get off my property or I'll shoot you down there where your brain is!" The house, the easement and the world trembled as she slammed the door. The spotlight lit his exit down the easement.

"Bitch!"

When she returned from work Monday evening, the easement was covered with a deep layer of thick, sharp gravel. Mr. Armstrong smiled as he sat in his recliner envisioning her maneuvering her high heels on the gravel. Tuesday afternoon, she drove up in her bright new car that went through the easement with a two inch space on either side as she slowly conquered the easement. The wheels of the car ground the gravel to a consistency of sand. She practiced diving in and out, in and out, in and out. Eventually, there were two ruts in the walkway that were easy, even with high heels. Mr. Armstrong's face was the most unbecoming shade of imperial red when she rolled down her window, smiled at him with "Howdy neighbor," as she turned onto the street and drove away in her spiffy little car.

When she returned from work on Thursday, the fencing lining the easement was now a seven foot wall. It was a tunnel. Undeterred, she drove through the tunnel with the ease most people drove major boulevards.

She decided it was propitious to befriend the neighbors on the other side of the easement . She became the godmother to one of the girls and "Mrs. K" to the teenage boys. She solidified her relationship with the family when she bought the young girl's quinceañera dress. They were easily convinced that Mr. Armstrong's easement wall was an affront to them as well as to her.

They were her friends for life. Mr. Armstrong was a shared enemy.

One Sunday morning, attempting to increase his, considerable, bulk, Mr. Armstrong inhaled as much air as his body would hold, before confronting her as she and I walked the easement toward the house. As we walked closer to him, she told me, in a strong loud voice, how amazingly, a pistol could equalize disputes between an average size woman and "fat bullies." When we were within a foot of him, she took a pistol from her purse and showed it to me. Not a word was said to him but, as we walked briskly past him, we heard and felt the explosion of air that left his body, reducing him to a little man who was paler than he was moments earlier. She smiled and waved to him as we turned toward the house. The next day, when she went out to clean away fallen avocados from his tree onto the grounds of the easement, Mr. Armstrong rushed out yelling, "Those are my avocados! Don't touch them!" He stepped closer, stood nose to nose with her and said "I've dealt with loudmouth bitches like you before, I know how to…"

Before he could finish his thought, she ripped her blouse open and in an operatic scream, pierced the air with "Rape! Rape! Rape!"

Within seconds, teenage boys came running to her rescue. No one saw how he managed to get away but he did. Mr. Armstrong disappeared behind his seven foot fence and became the neighborhood recluse who was rarely seen again.

Memories

BY REISS DUPLESSIS

"Hey Reiss, it's Barbara."

"Hi Barbara! How are ya?"

"I'm at the opera screening. Turn on your radio to KUSC and listen to the opera.

There is a young soprano singing 'Carmen' who reminds me of Rise Stevens. She's wonderful and she's only twenty-seven years old."

"Oh, OK. Will do. How are you feeling? Better?"

"Better! Talk to you later. Bye."

"OK. Bye."

Once tuned into the station on the radio, I hear the discussion. It's intermission at The Met. I take that moment to settle into my comfortable chair, facing the radio. Interesting, I think, how we face the radio almost like we expect to see as well as hear the broadcast. When the opera starts up again, I hear the beautiful opening music of the third act, one of my favorite interludes in all of the operatic repertoire. Very nice. The Met orchestra never fails to please. Eventually, the action brings us past the other characters to the sound of Carmen's voice. You know, instantly, when it's Carmen....the richness and depth of the voice and the music Bizet's written for it. After a few phrases I find myself exclaiming out loud, "Wow! What a voice." Barbara is right! I am hooked! The familiar music, that opera and tone of the mezzo's voice, do their magic and I am transported in time. I am, once again, a preteen boy, sitting on the brown floral flooring in our house in New Orleans, the house Mama did not like when we moved in. It was, she said, on the wrong side of the boulevard, the side her family never crossed.

I am alone in my world and thoughts. Mama and Baby Nell are doing their Saturday chores around the house. I am aware of them but my attention is focused on the music coming from the round speaker I can see outlined in the woven fabric on the front of the wondrous Stromberg Carlson radio, record player Baby Nell bought. She, supposedly, bought it for the family, for her enjoyment, for the house but, I know, with every fiber of my being, that she bought it for me! She ought it just for this... for me to sit on the floor in my own world, listening to the live broadcasts from the Metropolitan Opera in New York.

When I hear, "This is Milton Cross live from the Metropolitan Opera House in New York," I am in the fifth row of the opera house waiting for the curtain. From my warm spot on the floor, I can hear, feel and smell the audience around me. The orchestra starts the overture and all of my senses are tuned to the music and where it takes me.

Reveries. A long lifetime later, I can still remember, clearly, the magic of those Saturday mornings. I remember the comfort, the warmth, the happiness I enjoyed in that house with my sister, Baby Nell and Mama. Adele and Paul were married and Roy was rarely home. His boundless energy had him either at work or out with his friends. Those Saturday mornings were ours. Our house that Mama once hated was, now, the most comfortable place in the universe. On Saturday mornings, the aroma of Pine Oil took over after breakfast as Mama did her Saturday cleaning. Pine Oil was, evidently, her cleaning agent for everything. Well, there was also Bon Ami when we cleaned the windows. Oh, the windows.

Baby Nell worked on the outside while I worked on the inside. What great fun it was to simultaneously, apply the liquid white coat of Bon Ami to the glass and watch it dry to a white dull finish on the glass that made it impossible to see each other until, with the swipe of one finger, we could begin to see each other's smiling faces through the, suddenly, spotless, clean window pane. We'd, with our clean, dry cloth, wipe away the chalky cleaner until every inch of the glass was perfect. It was fun to point to spots we may have missed and figuring on who's side it was. There was, it seems, always a small streak in my side needing attention. After the windows were done it was time for the opera.

Mama and Baby Nell, often, did other chores while listening but I sat in my usual spot, on the floor, directly in front the large cabinet that housed the radio on one side and the fantastic record player on the other.

Of all the memories, the memories that colored my life, the memories that shaped my life, the memories that tattooed my life, the golden color of the air, the warmth of the rooms, the joyous understanding that these moments can never be erased, replaced or forgotten. Those Saturdays with my sister and my mother accompanied by the music from the Metropolitan Opera are among my most precious memories that continue, to this day, to convince me that mine has been a life blessed by the best humankind had to offer.

A Magical Drive

BY JERRY ELLINGSON

I stepped onto the porch brightened by the early morning sun. It was already warming the day. The cool breeze wafted across my face as I began to walk, ready to enjoy this glorious morning. When I reached the sidewalk, I knelt to retie my running shoe. My shoes hadn't run in a long, long time. At eighty-four, they were used for walking, and my walking had become slower and slower.

Having difficulty coming to a standing position, I reached over and put my hand on the trunk of a nearby tree to help me up. A large, black, shiny limousine pulled up to the curb. A chauffeur in a black uniform and black cap jumped out of the car and ran to help me. "Allow me, ma'am. We were just coming to pick you up. There's someone in the car waiting for you." I didn't even have time to say a word as he helped me to an upright position and opened the car door. I looked into the car in amazement, to see my mother smiling at me as she said, "We thought you might want to go for a ride."

"But you're….You can't be here." I stammered.

"Don't worry about that. Just come on in and give me a hug." I did just that and we talked and talked as the car began to drive away. "There are so many things I wanted to ask you after you were gone." I said. She smiled at me and softly said, "I know. We can talk on the way to pick up your brother."

"But he can't…. he isn't…." I protested.

"Don't worry about that. He's on a ship out on the ocean, of course. Where else would he be?" she said with a laugh.

The big, black limousine had reached the shore and just kept driving into the water. I stopped talking and looked out the window in dismay as it passed the breakwater and bobbed rhythmically over the swells on the ocean, moving towards the cargo ship out at sea.

"Don't be afraid," said my mother. "We're quite safe."

We approached the ship in no time. Dennis saw us, waved and began climbing down the rope ladder. The chauffeur opened the sunroof and Dennis dropped into the back with us. "Hi." He said, as if I had just seen him yesterday. We all began to talk and laugh.

When we reached the shore, the car stopped on the sand and the chauffeur jumped out, opened the door and I saw my dad standing there, smiling. I looked at my mother and said, "Are you okay with this? He hurt you a lot when he just left us." The smile never left her face as she answered, "Oh, yes. We see each other often." My dad got in and we all exchanged hugs and kisses.

The chauffeur looked back at us and asked, "Where to?" We all looked at each other. Then my brother answered, "Daddy, you always let us choose the road when we took long drives. This time, you get to choose." My dad thought for a minute, then he said, "Let's go to the mountains."

The car took off and was soon climbing higher and higher into the mountains. We passed forests and waterfalls. Although the road was winding, the ride was smooth and gentle. The car stopped once more, and my husband was waiting. I was in disbelief and beyond happy. He sat next to me, and we hugged and hugged. He said, "I tried to talk to you."

"I know. I heard you." I whispered.

We continued up to the top of the mountains. The car stopped. We all got out and looked over the beautiful world below. Finally, the chauffeur broke the quiet moment. "It's time to go back."

"Can we do this again, sometime?" I pleaded.

"No." my mother answered. "Next time this chauffeur will pick you up and bring you to us. This is Tommy."

I walked over to Tommy and said, "You look a little familiar. It's your eyes. Do I know you?"

"Yes," he said. "I'm Johnny's little brother. We lived across the street from you next to the Clarks. I always liked you. You let me play with you big kids even though I was a lot younger. You felt guilty your whole life because I died of polio. All your parents told you kids you shouldn't play in the ditch behind your house because you would catch polio. You played in the ditch anyway, and you let me play with you. That's not why I caught polio and it's not why I died. I have been waiting to be your chauffeur. I'll take good care of you."

"Can you tell me when you will be coming back?"

"No, but you still have some time."

Suddenly, I was standing on the sidewalk, my hand on the tree for support. The birds were singing, and the breeze was gently blowing and drying the tears on my face.

Light of NOW

by Eric Epstein

Please scan the QR code to view this unique poem that was created & performed in American Sign Language. This two-and-a-half-minute video features an ASL performer and some colorful backgrounds.

This ASL poem cannot be directly translated into English, but a general synopsis is provided in this blurb. In the beginning of the poem, the poet implores the audience to seize the present moment, with an imagery of Time himself flying off. Then, the poet tries to chase Time, leading to the realization that this moment is what's the most important. The poet then says that each moment is the same because they can be lived NOW. The poet lets go of past fixations and future wishes to focus on the shining glory of the present moment.

stock footage credit:
https://www.youtube.com/watch?v=ZeFpweKplHo
https://www.youtube.com/watch?v=I1Q2u7EnA2U
https://www.youtube.com/watch?v=cmqJskEqf9s

Hiroshima Haiku

BY BRYAN FRANCO

She gripped her basket
whilst foraging for mushrooms
then the plane flew by.

Why We Don't Irrigate Mango Trees with Salt Water

(A Tale Of Practiced Depression)

by Bryan Franco

Tears don't happen as easily these days.
I am not swallowing them.

I don't necessarily feel their presence in my thoughts,
yet I know they exist in my feelings, but sometimes,
my coping skills serve their purposes too well
when a torrent is warranted.

A good cry can be like running a 5K
after which I can feel both
exhausted and exhilarated.

Endorphins happen when tears
exit my soul as saline that feels
as if they should scald me.

Instead, they open my airways
allowing me to breathe as if I exist
in a meadow of mountain mint.

Tears exit my eyes wet and
find their way to dry leaving
salty residue upon my cheeks
and the edges of my lips.

While I am not partial to salty food,
I sometimes crave the taste of tears
as if they are made of mango juice.

I have never lifted a goblet of water to my lips expecting wine,
and tears will never taste of anything other than salt,
but allowing their existence allows for a future
with a potential for sweet.

The Final Renunciation of a Citizenship

BY BRYAN FRANCO

She stared at the home she was raised in:
a home her father carved from swampy woodland:
a place that should not feel foreign to her but did.

Her mother had passed three years prior from emphysema:
diagnosed over 30 years after quitting smoking.
Her father remained there.
She asked him to move in with her and the kids.
He declined.

He needed the familiarity of this structure
much of which came from trees on the land.
The wide-planked pecanwood floors
were a slight pinkish color that
qualified as muted rust.
The rough-hewn ponderosa pine walls
felt and looked like cedar
but smelled sweeter.

The porch railing which was originally metal was
replaced with crepe myrtle branches harvested
from trees her mom asked her dad to plant
that he crepe murdered four years later.
He committed crepe murder every other year since
and fashioned branches into canes he gave
as gifts to elderly friends and relatives
or sold at the church holiday bazaar.

This now empty home was a rebirth
of things taken from the land.
Now empty of both her parents,
furniture, and bric-a-brac,
she relinquished its future
to a real estate agent.

She walked across the floors.
She ran her fingers along the walls.
The stairs still had a tell-tale squeak
on the fourth-to-last step.

After she realized the hand-scrolled molding
in her childhood bedroom was a love letter from
father to daughter, its memory sweetened
her sleeping dreams for years.

Incarnations of Beaches

BY BRYAN FRANCO

When I walk the beach, apparitions of my former self often
walk with me.

Five-year-old me fills his hands with sandy mud and lets it
escape through his fingers.

Seven-year-old me draws a crooked line through wet sand
with his big toe. He walks at tide's edge; warm Gulf of
Mexico water rushes over his feet.

Eight-year-old me writes his name in the same sand with
the same big toe.

Ten-year-old me plays Frisbee with his brothers who catch
it every time; he doesn't stop smiling despite that he rarely
catches the Frisbee himself.

Teenage me ponders jumping off the Alabama Point Bridge
because so many others say they've done it.

Twenty-one-year-old me, who bikes twenty miles
four days a week, refuses to remove his trunks at
a California nude beach.

Twenty-five-year old me walks alone on a winter day and
marvels at stark gray winter sky against white sand and
turquoise water. He laughs at a joke his father once
told him; he can't stop laughing because no one
could tell a joke like dad.

One month prior, he had recited Kaddish as he tossed fresh dirt atop a wooden casket with shiny brass rails. In another year, he will place a rock upon his father's gravestone.

A forty-four-year-old me draws a long straight line
through wet sand with his big toe.
He walks at tide's edge; cold Atlantic water rushes over his feet.
He wonders why he hasn't been to a beach in over four years.

Friends

by Nan Friedley

In 1994, I met six twenty
somethings living in New York
I joined them as they maneuvered
love, careers, and relationships
I was introduced to them in
episode one at their coffee shop
        neatnik chef Monica
        Chandler a wannabe joker
        fashionista Rachel
        Ross, paleontologist divorcee
        soap opera actor Joey and
        Phoebe, singer/songwriter of
            "Smelly Cat"

After eight years and ten seasons
we became best friends, ones that I
can find almost anytime, day or night
on Hulu or Peacock or Nick at Nite, thank
goodness for reruns

RIP Chandler

Hello Goodbye

BY NAN FRIEDLEY

in anticipation, my 12-year
old self moved a chair, close
to the family's chunky console
black and white TV, channel set
on CBS, waiting for the 8:00 hour
the start of this special Ed Sullivan
Show on Sunday night, February 9, 1964

it was the beginning of
Long and Winding Road, first
performance in America for a
screaming crowd who couldn't
Help themselves. It was A Day
In the Life I'll remember always
Here, There and Everywhere

Do You Want to Know a Secret
saved my weekly allowance to buy
their latest forty-five, each one would
only Please, Please Me more
until they Let It Be and
couldn't Get Back, the four
guys went their separate ways
Ob-la-di, Ob-la-da life goes on

Purrfect

BY NAN FRIEDLEY

being the runt, I can squeeze under the footstool to
catch a nap in the afternoon or pull open the linen
closet door with my paw to snooze among the towels
and sheets or get stuck in the tiny space between the
kitchen cupboard and the wall…

rescued when I meowed
loud enough to be found
in my dusty hiding hole

CANCER

by Nan Friedley

Polyp
waited to be more
lurked in the dark colonic
space, fed its hungry cells
grew into a greedy mass
hard, cancerous cells multiplied
piled onto each other pushing
filled any empty space into
the lining and beyond
seeking more nearby
demanding, invading
Tumor

Googler

seems I have too much time on my hands
waiting for CT scan, ultrasound, colonoscopy
results, giving me time to wonder, time to worry
time to want to know more

as time goes on, my questions
evolve…meandering on a dark path
lead me to more wondering
more worry about

how many symptoms do I have?
will surgery make me cancer-free?
what does stage 2A mean?
will I need chemo?
will I survive long enough to find the
        answers?

☁ Cottonball Clouds and Claps of Thunder

BY CAMILLE GAON

Marshmallow clouds
With whipped meringue swirls

Are Cumulus clouds that line up like a string of pearls
Cotton balls and whipped cream

Drop unique flakes of snow
From flattened as pancakes Stratus clouds that always lay low

Wispy clouds like angel hair
Are Cirrus clouds that ensure weather that's fair

Cumulonimbus clouds bring thunder and hail
If you have a leaky roof
You better grab a pale

Daydreams sleep on these cushions in the sky
So, keep your head in the clouds if you don't want time to fly

Residing in Limbo

BY CAMILLE GAON

It's not fun residing here,
A gun to my head, causing fear

Is it lymphoma or recurrent cancer
I guess I appreciate this limbo of not knowing the answer

Normally I don't like to wait
But this time, I'm not in a hurry to know my fate

So, for now I'm going to amp up and live my life to the hilt
And toss thoughts of worry, regret and uncertainty away with guilt

Because right now in this moment
I'm feeling fine

And I'm going to treasure the present of the present and hope
    that it's all going to be benign

Temporary Housing, Residing in Uncertainty

BY CAMILLE GAON

Ignorance is bliss, so I've just this last week moved into a delightful short-term rental home with lush gardens on Bliss Blvd whilst awaiting some biopsy results from a procedure done four days ago.

I expect to be staying in this charming abode until the test results are in sometime towards the middle to the end of next week. Some people hate the waiting and I am usually one of them, but this time there were so many indicators of this not being the desired "breathe a sigh of relief" news that I am contented as a bird in her cozy nest, high up in a fragrant orange tree, just waiting here and enjoying the sun, the moon, the view and the safety of the ignorance in this holding pattern.

I've learned to make friends with uncertainty over the years and also somehow, against all odds, I've just this week learned what it is to be truly patient. A trait I've never for an instant possessed.

So, I shall embrace the now of not being in the know and make some nurturing delicious orange juice if the news is delivered with nothing more than a twist of bitter lemon. Admittedly, I have very deep-rooted issues with control and whilst I can't steer the outcome of these biopsies in the direction that I would like them to go, I can take the high road and control my reaction or overreaction and steer myself away from the darkness of a bumpy dirt road and onto a sunny, smoothly paved highway.

Booted off Bliss Blvd

BY CAMILLE GAON

December 7, 2023

As expected, I was given the anticipated eviction notice today that I'd have to vacate my charming cottage of temporary housing on Bliss Blvd, where I resided in ignorance for 9 joyful days whilst awaiting my groin lymph node biopsy results.

I knew what they'd be, but it was a sweet self-indulgent treat to live pleasantly in "Let's Pretendville" for even such a short duration.

Now faced with the conundrum of where to move, I weighed my choices. Cancer Carousel Court, Medical-Merry-Go-Round Road, Radical Radiation Road, Laser-guided Proton Place, Surgery Street, Alternative Avenue or Denial Drive?

None of the most popular offerings were really options for me given my unique drug sensitivities, prior radiation in the area to disqualify proton therapy and Surgery Street was out because it was hard to get a doctor to remove the one, lone affected lymph node. Their protocol was "all or nothing."

My answer to that was, "Hit the road, Jack. Ass." I don't want to be left with no immune system.

The medical merry-go-round was looking rather like a neighborhood that was too congested with aggravation, chasing one's tail and plus, I'd lived there for almost 15 years looking over my shoulder for another recurrence, thus robbing me of the present of enjoying "the present." I ruled this option out pretty quickly knowing that parking was an issue.

I can't entertain for a minute relocating to Denial Drive, since I've always been one to address challenges head on, so I'm making the move to Alternative Avenue. Fingers crossed that the neighbors will be nice and I'll be able to get rid of the weeds in the front yard.

Free at Last

by Ragini Goel

I dreamt
I was crawling
on a mulberry tree,
feasting on leaves,
so fresh and so green.
Not a creature around,
no worries, no fear
I ate and ate till
my tummy was full.
I took a big burp
and yawned out aloud,
stretching arms so wide
as wide as I could.
I then wrapped myself
in a blanket, my own
and quietly snuggled
into my silky cocoon.
I dozed off to sleep
and sank into slumber,
a slumber so deep,
no worries, no fear.
Not a thing could I hear
so deep was my sleep.
When my slumber was done
I woke up all fresh
to a beautiful dawn
of fulfilled dreams.
I yearned to be free,
And craved to explore,
the world on my own.
I found I have wings
colorful and golden

big spotted wings,
bright orange and black,
my beautiful wings!
I then flew away
with tears in my eyes
waving goodbye to
the mulberry tree,
my home, my shelter
my bed, my canopy!
I took off with glee
like a monarch I was,
a mighty monarch,
Regal and free!
Free to roam
wherever I please,
free to reign the
Whole world supreme!

My Librarian

BY RAGINI GOEL

Ms. Grace, my librarian
quietly sporting
her own demeanor,
wearing, the usual,
her blue gingham dress,
hair tucked in a bun,
a neat little bun
the bun shrinking
away with each
passing year,
hair growing gray
glasses, thicker,
thicker each year
her face showing
rugged pathways
of life's journeys,
frailer and thinner
as time goes by
droopy in posture
knees worn out from
climbing ladders
arms getting weary
reaching for shelves
shelves too long for her
lean frame to access,
smiles and asks me
how many books
you want my dear?
She knows I'm greedy,
greedy for books.
I always want more
a whole lot more

more than I can chew.
She knows that
she knows that well
she also knows
the right words to say
she tells me
I am ambitious.
"Really Ambitious,"
as she stamps the date
the date to return
my pile of books
struggling to fit into
my torn tote bag!

When I Was Little (Little Did We Know)

BY MILAN HAMILTON

When I was little there were cows
And farmers milking them with their hands.
When I was little my uncles all went to war
But all I saw were pictures of them in their uniforms.
When I was little there were no cowboys,
Except in the movies every Saturday.
When I was little war was on the screen too,
But never as a horror movie.
When I was little, little did I know
Milk would come from industrialized cows,
And athletes who never learned to milk a cow
Would be paid more than farmers,
And politicians acting like preschoolers
Would suck up all the airwaves
While the suffering and dying continue
From all the bad decisions and hatreds
Continuing on from when I was little—
But little did I know.

Sonnetizing

BY MILAN HAMILTON

A sonnet is an awesome, splendid way (A)
To enter into life's mysterious depths (B)
With verses sweet and full of sunshine's rays (A)
Or heavy with love's agonies bereft. (B)
Oh William, can you guide this trembling hand? (C)
It's venturing where it has never been. (D)
To write a sonnet seemed a natural plan, (C)
But now uncertainty says "hello friend." (D)
An iamb seemed so simple all alone, (E)
But when some words are added in such form (F)
Pentameter makes difficulty loom— (E)
Is this to be our fate, be left forlorn? (F)
Not so, dear bard, this vessel still aright (G)
Will guide this trembling hand to write. (G)

Sonnet AD 2022

BY MILAN HAMILTON

Another January's promise came
But February brought new violence
In March the god of war's refrain
Drowned out the showers of April's innocence.
Our daughter's visit made our month May
In June we marked the years at forty-four.
July brought heat we thought had come to stay;
Through August temperatures were seen to soar.
September marked by sadness, a young man's death
In October, Redlands got its Arrow Train.
Our Republic in November caught its breath.
A gift in December, when our granddaughter came.
Oh! Anno domini 2022!
A mixed bag you were! But we're thankful for you!

My Life as a Seed

BY MILAN HAMILTON

I once went hunting pheasant.
Shot one—beautiful!
The pheasant—not the shot—
Gave up hunting on the spot.

Spent summers on the farm
To escape the city life,
Only for the summer,
Missed my city friends.

Loved the farm—but farming?
That was not for me.
My life was spent in cities—
Was that my destiny?

Now knowing what I know,
And seeing what I see,
Will I become a gardener,
Or just a planted seed?

It's just a question posed,
The answer eludes me.
My life will serve its purpose
If I can be the seed.

Acts of Kindness

BY MILAN HAMILTON

Are not always
What they seem.
Can an act appear
To be that kind
Yet destroy a dream?
Or is an act unkind
When first received
A blessing in disguise?
A pink slip
Delivered by phone
May open new doors
Of possibility
For acts of kindness
Received and given,
Offer the chance
To say, "You are worthy!"
Or "I love you!"
My neighbors' knocks
Are always kind
When sharing baked delights.
I shared tomatoes
From my garden
Kind of kind, I guess.
I keep pocket cash
Just in case
I meet Jesus walking.
I turn the compost
In my garden, attempting
To be kind to Mother Earth.
Acts of kindness or not—
Not for me to judge—
Opportunity knocks.

Ode to an Unknown Flower

by Milan Hamilton

A flower caught my attention
As I hurried along a path
It seemed to wave hello
I stopped a moment—listened—
Waited for a sign—none came.
That flower only waved it's greeting
For any passing stranger's viewing;
Then why was I the lucky one,
This day—this morn—this moment,
To receive this special greeting
From an unknown floral being
And feel my life undone.

Querida Mamita Cándida

by Dora Harmon

Mi amiga, Frances Vásquez te trajo a mi mente y estoy muy feliz de recordarte, abuela, porque hacen tantos y tantos años que te fuiste a tu verdadero hogar. Siguen vivos en mi memoria los recuerdos de una época donde todo era amor, paz, y felicidad — donde tú nos contabas historias de tu vida en el campo: ordeñando vacas; jugando en el riachuelo cerca de la casa; trepando a los árboles; haciendo toda clase de inocente travesuras; y, más tarde, como fue el conocer a mi abuelo y casarte. Recuerdo que a pesar de ser una mujer muy religiosa, y en aquella época (100 años atrás) donde la mujer era un cero a la izquierda, tú nos hablabas de orgullo y dignidad; de respeto hacia los demás; y, de la misma manera exigirlo hacia nosotras — no sumisión ni aceptar la esclavitud.

Eras rezandera —lo que no te impedía ser alegre y bailarina. Tu hija (mi madre) heredó tu filosofía de vida (pero no era tan rezandera) y yo también heredé tu filosofía de vida multiplicada — menos lo de rezandera. Yo cambie la religiosidad por espiritualidad. Ha sido maravilloso, Mamita Cándida, traerte a mi memoria y pensar que llegará el día en que en un mundo mejor nos encontraremos de nuevo. Hasta entonces, preciosa abuela, con amor, tu nieta Dora.

Acerca de Mi Madre

by Dora Harmon

Mi mama, Elisa Giraldo, fué un ser humano maravillo y muy estricta. Todas sus órdenes la cumplíamos al pie de la letra, desde la servidumbre hasta la mayor de sus hijas, yo. Fuímos ocho hermanos y hermanas y a pesar de que ella trabajaba con mi padre en un supermercado grande que tenía enseguida de la casa, siempre estuvo presente y con mucho amor. Tenia ella dos señoras de servicio: una para atender la casa y la otra para atender los niños. Ha si que, aunque trabajaba mucho, siempre estaba a metros de distancia y con un policía vigilante (nuestra nana) que a la menor infracción, avisaba inmediatamente al "general con falda" (mi amada madre). Y era completamente legal agarrar a correazos al "delincuente" — ha si fuera por una infracción menor. A nosotros los hijos nos parecía normal que ha si fuera y que no tuviésemos la más mínima libertad para ir solas a ninguna parte o decidir acerca de nada.

Hoy en día me parece maravilloso que ha si haya sido, porque tuvimos una niñez maravillosa y una juventud pletórica de paz, armonía y felicidad — sin los problemas que se presentan cuando los niños tienen relaciones con el sexo opuesto y toman decisiones sin tener la madures o la capacidad para hacerlo. Éramos una familia muy grande, ha si que con mi mama y con mi papa que en ocasiones se nos unía. Íbamos a todas las fiestas que se nos presentaban y ha si era como tan pronto aprendíamos a caminar; aprendíamos a bailar y quizás esto tenga que ver con el hecho que aun hoy en día a mis 83 años de edad, el baile sea para mí, prioridad número uno en mi vida.

Hasta los 18 años no nos fue permitido tener amigos o novios, pero a pesar de tener 18 años, no podíamos salir sola con ellos. Ellos eran bienvenidos en nuestra casa, siempre y cuando el "general" estuviese presente. Mi mama era una mujer muy bonita, muy elegante y muy orgullosa. Recuerdo que cuando llego la moda de los pantalones para las mujeres, mi mama inmediatamente se los puso y a mi papa, por poco le da un ataque cardiaco, al ver a su esposa vestida como un macho y el ejemplo que le estaba dando a sus hijas. Lo mismo paso con el labial rojo, mi mama me conto que recién casados, mi papa le botaba el labial, pero ella compraba otro y lo ponía en el mismo lugar — no había razón para esconderlo. Él tenia que aprender a respetar sus gustos y así fue siempre. A mi "general", ni mi papa le pudo imponer órdenes. A pesar de haber nacido en un hogar Católico y en una época donde las mujeres debían ser tan sumisas y obedientes como borregos sin vos ni voto, en ningún aspecto, ella no fue así. Su hija mayor (yo) resulto tener exactamente la misma personalidad y carácter.

Otro aspecto de su personalidad era su sensibilidad hacia los mas necesitados, no recuerdo cual era la enfermedad que tenia mi hermana (la segunda), pero mi mama la llevaba al hospital a un tratamiento. Siempre me llevaba a mi con ella y después de dejarla con el médico, compraba desayuno para los mendigos que había en la acera del hospital — y quedo grabada en mi mente la imagen de un anciano con sus piernas llenas de llagas y mi mama se agallaba a darle el desayuno. También recuerdo que cuando un mendigo llegaba a la casa a pedir limosna lo cual era normal. Si estábamos en la mesa, tenían que permitirle la entrada al mendigo y acomodarlo en la mesa para comer con nosotros, sin importar que tan sucio y harapiento estuviera. Mi madre era supremamente alegre, cordial, positiva, y le gustaba mucho bailar y cantar porque tenia una bonita voz. Ella nunca estuvo enferma en un hospital — disfrutó de una salud maravillosa y no sé si será cuestión de genes o el alto grado de positivismo y vida armoniosa y feliz, porque yo, a mis 84 abriles, tampoco he tenido nunca ninguna enfermedad.

Mi madre partió a los 93 años de edad cuando dormía, a si que se fue tan feliz como vivió, dejando a sus hijos grandes enseñanzas de amor al trabajo, honestidad, orgullo y dignidad, respeto y compasión por los demás y el perecedero recuerdo de una vida plena y feliz a su lado. Sobre todo a sus hijas nos enseño con palabras y hechos ha hacernos respetar de todos los hombres a nuestro alrededor, quizás sea la razón por la cual me he casado tres veces y el último sigue conmigo, porque es un angelito — de lo contrario, ya lo hubiese devuelto al mercado.

Mi Jardín Secreto

by Dora Harmon

Es mi mente un maravilloso jardín secreto, donde la paz, la serenidad y la armonía, sirven de ambiente para disfrutar una vida tan llena de actividades, todas escogidas por mi y para mi felicidad. Son muchos los dones que disfruto en esta época de mi vida: la capacidad de disfrutar lo que se tiene sin lagrimas ni añoranzas por lo que no se tiene; una salud física, mental y emocional envidiable, un ángel de carne y hueso en casa que me quiere, me trata como una reina, y la libertad que yo disfruto en esta época de mi vida.

Aunque no me molestó trabajar, lo hice por 60 años y acabo de descubrir lo maravilloso que es la libertad, ir solamente a donde quiera, cuando quiera, viajar por todo el mundo sin limites de tiempo, tomar un libro en las mañanas y leer hasta que me canse; ir a bailar cuando se me antoje, recibir clases de pintura, regresar al colegio a estudiar a mis 50 años de edad. ¡Es fantástico! No he podido saciar el hambre de saber, de aprender y de conocer, lo cual me lleva a toda clase de conferencias y es precisamente el hambre intelectual lo que me motiva a este constante ir y venir, esto es lo que hace mi vida interesante y feliz.

Vivo exactamente en el lugar del mundo donde quiero vivir y en la casa que quiero vivir, rodeada de un hermoso jardín, pájaros, fuentes de agua y peces. ¡Es mi paraíso! Dios mío, no tengo nada que pedirte, solo puedo agradecer tantas bendiciones — sobre todo mi mente que me da la fortaleza para arrancar, como el rastrojo de mi jardín, disgustos, frustraciones, sueños no realizados y perdidas; mirando solo las cosas positivas y maravillosas que hay a mi alrededor. Siempre oí decir que la vejez era horrible, pero para mí la percepción normal de la vejez no existe. Existe la tercera juventud puede ser tan maravillosa y excitante como la primera o segunda ronda, y todo depende absolutamente de la capacidad que tengamos para lograr que así sea.

Actitud

by Dora Harmon

ENTRE MÁS VIVO, más me doy cuenta del impacto que la actitud tiene en la vida. La actitud para mi es más importante que los hechos; es más importante que el pasado, la educación, el dinero — que las circunstancias, que los fracasos, los éxitos. Es más importante que lo que la gente piensa, dice, o hace.

La actitud es más importante que la apariencia, capacidades que se tengan, o conocimientos. La actitud buena o mala puede levantar o quebrar una empresa, una iglesia, un hogar. Pero lo más maravilloso es que está en nuestras manos el decidir, cada día y a cada momento, qué actitud tomar hacia lo que nos toque enfrentar en la vida. Nosotros no podemos cambiar el pasado. No podemos cambiar el hecho de que la gente hable o actúe como lo hace. Nosotros no podemos cambiar lo inevitable. Lo único que podemos hacer es controlar lo que está a nuestro control ha si que, lo único que podemos hacer es controlar lo que está bajo nuestro control… Ll actitud que tomamos hacia las circunstancias de la vida. Estoy convencida que el Edén o el infierno en nuestras vidas, depende de un 10% de lo que nos pasa y un 90% en como reaccionamos hacia lo que nos pasa. Nosotros estamos en control de nuestra actitud y por lógica hacia nuestra felicidad.

Neutralizando pensamientos negativos: cada uno de nosotros tiene el poder y la habilidad para tomar el total y completo control de nuestras vidas para neutralizar lo que tu quieras neutralizer, y crear lo que tu quieras crear. Los que creen que no pueden hacerlo y se sienten sin el poder para controlar sus vidas, son los que están ciegos, solo temporalmente por la máscara de la cuarta dimensión física de la realidad. La verdad es que eres capaz y que estas listo para hacerlo. Neutralizar la energía negativa, puede verse como un proceso de desintoxicación. Cargamos muchos conceptos erróneos de miedos, dudas, iras, odios y mil cosas más

— acumuladas en el trascurso de nuestras vidas que nos ciegan acerca de quienes somos realmente, y nos tienen prisioneros de la miseria y de las dificultades, impidiéndonos, para manifestar lo que realmente somos y merecemos.

Aférrate, cree en ello: visualízalo hecho realidad en tu mente todos los días a cada momento y su imagen mental se materializará. Porque cuando esperas lo mejor, desarrollas una fuerza mental magnética que por una ley de atracción, te traerá lo mejor.

A Special Friendship: Tree and Squirrel

BY CONNIE JAMESON

A chill in the air made Tree feel sad. With fall and winter's cold weather, his beautiful green leaves would soon be gone. They would turn yellow, orange and brown, become dry and fall to the ground. Tree's trunk and branches would be left stark and bare and. . . ugly. No longer would people come to enjoy and appreciate the shade his leaves provided on hot, sunny days.

Tree would miss the children playing beneath his branches and all the families and friends having picnics. The fun of having a bird nest in his branches — the laying and hatching of eggs, noisy little babies' hungry calls, busy parents traveling to and fro to provide food — these activities had ended. Those little baby birds grew up and flew away. That unneeded, unused nest became weathered and wasted away and was now gone from his branches.

"Hey, what's wrong?" Someone had noticed Tree looking sad and forlorn. Oh, it was that new squirrel he had seen running around the park recently. "Well, hello, little fellow. Sorry, but I've been thinking about the months that lie ahead. I dread standing here with my bare branches feeling useless and forgotten. Look at those evergreen trees out there in the distance. I wish I could be more like them. They are green and beautiful all year long. Me? I know I'll just be plain and ugly in the months ahead."

"Whoa now, Mr. Tree, listen to me. I'm new in your park, but I've seen trees like you other places. You will not look ugly in the winter months. Actually, without your leaves, people will see your strong, stately trunk and the beautiful designs of your branches. When snow or ice covers your branches, they are even more striking. You help make those days ahead a 'Winter Wonderland.' People will come to admire you."

"Another thing, Mr. Tree. You are not useless, at least not to me. When dogs are chasing and scaring me, you provide a safe place to escape, whether you have leaves or not. Also, I appreciate that handy little hole way up there in your trunk. That's where I've hidden some nuts to provide food when it's hard to find. You are really a good friend to me, Mr. Tree."

"Oh, Squirrel, you are my special friend, too. You are helping me see the good, the positives, about just being me and to appreciate all the times of the year. I'm so glad you are now living here in my park. Thank you, Squirrel."

Time to Rhyme

BY CONNIE JAMESON

Hey, want to try your hand at poetry?
Seriously! You're asking me?

It's a great class; instructor's the best.
Oh, come on now, surely you jest!

I'll tell you all about it; let's have a chat.
Poetry — let me tell you — I never do that.

Listen — I know your writing is really quite clever.
Maybe so, but me worry about rhymes — never!

At end of each line just put a rhyming word.
Personally now, I find that quite absurd.

You don't have to worry; they don't give a grade.
No! I wouldn't do it, even if I got paid.

Ah, do I sense you might have a little fear?
I'm not afraid; let that be perfectly clear.

Or maybe you're just a little lazy?
No, I think rhyming is just plain crazy!

Come on, ol' pal, do it with me.
No, my friend, that will never be.

Give it a try.
I'd rather die.

So?
NO!

Ode to a Junk Drawer

BY MARGO KLEIN

"Thou still unravished bride of quietness,
Thou foster child of silence and slow time,
Sylvan historian, who canst thus express
A flowery tale more sweetly than our rhyme"

What shapes abound in my fair junk drawer,
"What mad pursuit? What struggle to escape?"
The luscious, translucent glowing of metal keys,
Of paper clips, of yesterday's twist ties.
Where lurks the uncapped pens, the pencil stubs?
Scraps of paper lie like snowcapped waves
Among the chaos of debris.

And yet, three treasures lie within, waiting to be,
Hoping to be freed, to fly out of the drawer into a
Willing hand. The first gleams like sunshine,
Pure and useful: the scotch tape.
Hidden deeper is the second, a more bucolic fellow,
Humble and papery: the masking tape.
Ye gods, the third is a wonderful thing indeed,
Highly prized, highly praised, for it be duct tape.

The joys, the subtleties, the beauty of this fair drawer,
Embodies all of life.
"Beauty is truth, truth beauty-that is all
Ye know on earth, and all ye need to know."

My Life as a Chocolate Chip

BY MARGO KLEIN

I started life on a cacao plantation in Africa. Since a cacao tree has up to 2,000 pods and each pod has 30 to 40 cacao beans, I had plenty of brothers and sisters to keep me company. The first big event in my life was when my pod was harvested and I was removed by hand from the pod. This is similar to the teenage years for a human. I was young and bitter, but after fermentation, I was cleaned and roasted. Now, considerably sweeter, I was ready to pursue my career.

A long journey across the ocean gave me and my siblings and cousins time to muse on our futures. Some, of course, held the highest ambitions, Ghirardelli and Godiva was all they could talk about. Others were lazy and unfocused, we knew they would wind up in dollar store cookies or chocolates, and they seemed fine with that.

For my part, I had only one dream from the time I was a little nib: I wanted to be a chocolate chip. And not any old chocolate chip, I didn't want to be part of a chocolate chip muffin or chocolate chip ice cream. No, no, no. My dream was a warm, sweet, slightly soft chocolate chip cookie.

The excitement of graduation day drew near, when we would be loaded onto various trucks and rail cars. Finally, we docked. We could all hear the load manager calling out the destinations for the crates. Godiva was first off, followed by Ghirardelli and Hershey's, next came a slew of house brands I'd never heard of. I'd almost given up hope when the grappling hook lifted my crate to the shout of Nestle.

During the truck ride to the processing plant, I prayed that I wouldn't be chosen to be a chocolate bar or a Kit Kat. You cannot imagine my feeling of satisfaction as I was shaped and packaged in the iconic yellow bag with the tollhouse cookie on the front.

But my life was not yet complete, I waited anxiously as I was delivered to the grocery store and I struggled to keep my package wrinkle free as I was placed on the shelf. Now the waiting, so stressful, as I fought my anxiety about my fate. Then, the day came when a mother with her twins picked up my bag while talking about the school fundraiser I was bound for. Oh, life is sweet. My future is all I dreamed of and more! A luscious treat to be savored and I would raise money for a worthy cause. No one has had a better life than I have!

If Only

BY MARGO KLEIN

If only my friend would have been on time, my life would have been completely different.

I was sitting in the lobby of a Washington, D.C. hotel waiting for a friend. She was coming to town with the chorus group from her college for a performance. I had met her back in high school and we'd kept in touch. This would be the first time we'd met up in person in several years.

Time was dragging by slowly and I was killing time by people watching. I had noticed a group of three soldiers who also seemed to be waiting for someone, and they seemed to have also noticed me. One of the men peeled off and headed my way. "Can I be of any help? You seem to be abandoned over here?" Maybe not the best pickup line, but he was cute. I explained that my friend was over an hour late at this point and I was considering just going back home. He sat down and we talked for about ten minutes before he had to leave with his friends. My phone number left in his pocket. We've been married now for over 50 years and I consider him the best thing that ever happened to me.

As for my friend, she arrived later, almost two hours after the appointed time. The police had picked up her and her choral group for trying to sing illegally at the Lincoln Memorial. They didn't know they needed a permit. A misdemeanor for her and a marriage for me.

Humpty Dumpty

BY MARGO KLEIN

This is Channel One coming to you live with breaking news. I am here at the scene of a tragic occurrence that just happened a short while ago. It has been confirmed that Humpty Dumpty was sitting on a wall and had a great fall. We have heard that all the king's men could not put Humpty Dumpty together again.

The question of course is whether this was an accident, perhaps Mr. Dumpty fainted in the heat or misjudged the distance. It could also be a suicide. He was reported to be depressed over the falling price for eggs. But detectives are looking into whether this is a homicide. It has been rumored that Humpty Dumpty had a lot of enemies.

Here, to give us an exclusive statement is Mr. Big Bad Wolf.

Were you acquainted with the deceased and do you have any comments?

"Of course, I knew him, he was always sitting on that wall smirking. He made many of us angry here in Nursery Town."

And why was that Mr. Bad Wolf?

"Well just listen to you, calling me a bad wolf. Everyone always called him 'A good egg.' It made plenty of us villain types outraged. But I didn't push him, if you ask me, he scrambled his own brains."

Okay, thank you Mr. Bad er Just Wolf.

It's been a really hot day and I see some fried egg pieces here on the sidewalk, oh wait, here come four and twenty blackbirds. That should play havoc with the evidence, and I see Little Jack Horner approaching with his spoon. No, no, the king's men are turning him back and chasing the blackbirds. The evidence is being preserved. I only have time for one more quick interview.

What do you make of this case, Sir?

"My name is Sherlock Holmes. It is my business to know what other people do not know. I say, the butler did it."

Elegy Written in an Upstairs Room
While Listening to the Band

BY ROBIN LONGFIELD

Richard Manuel's voice, ethereal
through the white Bose speaker–
"All things lost are found with you"
what did he find at the well–
despair or something deeper?

All love is a transition
from there to here to nowhere–
Its energy immortal
Immutable, but beware
of seeking truth or visions
in that brilliant burning light--
some will emerge, triumphantly

while others just burn bright–
burn bright, but not as diamonds
but opals, their fire encased–
forever trapped forever
burning at the horizon,
a sunset never erased

by time or discovery
of all that once was lost
was this true for you, Richard
too delicate for beauty's fire
or oblivious of its cost?

What called to you
that night in Winter Park–
was it "Whispering Pines"
through curtains, your voice
a Charon's boat into the dark?

II

Oceano drowned
in the rains
of December–homes
taken to the sea
returned as found objects
delicate, broken, remnants
tangled in seaweed.

The dunes collapsed
on themselves, washed away–
stables gone, horses

evacuated, people
evacuated, trailers

moved to higher ground.

III

Higher ground
is what I sought for you
beautiful, departed
child of mine

I wanted to love away
all that was lost within you
before the flood that carried

you from all horizons
wept at its hideous duty.

I wanted to be
a star
letting in light
into your endless night.

I wanted to be a wave
that could smooth away
your brokenness
the way the ocean
smoothes broken bottles
into sea glass,
leaves flecks of gold
around scallop shells.

I wanted to see
beauty in what was left
at low tide–
beauty in what was left.

I wanted to be
your mother.

IV

Your leaving
was another transition
love's labor lost forever–

time
sweetens harmonies—
weary voices singed
with bourbon and smoke
testify universal truths–

whose voice
do I hear tonight?

Beside the Bose speaker,
a white candle burns bright
tonight–-
bright for you, dear Mia
and for Richard Manuel—

a white candle burning bright
on this dark, December night.

The Book of Old Bats

BY ROBIN LONGFIELD

What do you do when you are an old Bat?

You can go to the Theater
In your best old bat hat,

Hang out in the rafters
With Debbie and Dave

Have a savory snack later
At the Au' Bat Cafe

Where the bugs are all chubby
And served on a plate

There's no need for hunting
And there's never a wait

You can visit museums
On Free Old Bat Nights

Or the Batco Arena
To watch the Bat fights.

You can go to the park
And hang out in the trees

With your best Bat friend Amy
Or Catherine Louise

To catch up on Bat gossip
And tell Tall Bat Tales,

The taller the better,
Gigantic as whales!

You could go shopping for jewelry
Or a shiny black cape,

In the softest of velvet
Instead of dull crepe.

You can look after Grandbaby bats
And their wild echolocation

Or you can just say "Not Now"
And go on a long, long vacation

To the land of old Bats
Who are looking for fun

It might be Bat Vegas
Or the land of no sun.

You can act quite outrageous,
You can act coy and shy

You can stay home if you want
 You can eat, drink, and fly

To wherever you like
And as long as you wish

To be an old Bat,
Is especially this—

You can be who you want
Be it fancy or plain

But the happiest old Bats
Never complain or explain!

That is the secret
When you are an old Bat

Just be who you are,
And that, little batlings, is that!

A Cinco De Mayo Celebration
(Drabble)

BY MERRILL LYEW

The couple agreed on celebrating Cinco de Mayo with friends.

"As a Mexican celebration, we should have a barbecue evening with carne asada and taquitos," she said.

He argued that they were living in the USA, and it should be patties with buns.

After not finding common ground, both freelancers returned to their laptops, and continued with their work.

The days went by. Their guests showed up on their doorsteps. The couple had forgotten all about the barbecue. No provisions were made for the evening.

He drove immediately to a popular taco stand to get enough carne asada and taquito.

Portland to San Bernardino 1988

BY ANNE MALCOLM

Jan glanced at Sean for reassurance. The blue light of the IHOP sign glowed in his face, turning his tan skin pallid. The Portland night was cold. Wind whipped trash rose and spiraled back to earth in the gusty wind. It seemed too seedy a strip mall for such a meeting. Odors of rotting garbage seeped from the alley. Sean squeezed Jan's hand. Reassured, she continued forward with him. They were a team, they would do this together. Buoying one another up along this mutually chosen path.

The inner doors, into the restaurant's foyer, opened as they approached the glass outer doors. A small child toddled through. Jan's heart leapt. The child was beautiful. "It's her" she blurted, even as her mind registered the impossibility of knowing such a thing. The couple halted abruptly watching the child. Ever aware of one another, and moving in tandem.

Delight had registered on the child's face as the doors opened magically releasing her. Sensing freedom, she ran through them into the lobby space, wide eyed. She was curious, thrilled by her escape. She caught sight of the automatic newspaper vending machines, and approached them, pulling at their handles and peering in at the front page pictures. She investigated the machines, one by one. The couple watched, enthralled. No one followed the child. "It's her," Jan said again. "How can you possibly know?" he teased with a smile. He knows too, she thought and smiled back.

The child turned to approach the restaurant's outer doors. They whooshed open welcoming her to the grimy parking lot. She moved forward. Jan broke towards her. The child startled, seeing a stranger approaching fast. The toddler turned and ran back towards the inner doors. Sensing her, the doors whooshed open again, allowing entrance back into the humid air of the restaurant. Jan and Sean followed at a distance, laughing and watching.

The child had unilaterally decided the pair would be her new friends in a game of hide-and-seek. Frequently looking back to check the smiling strangers were following, she toddled to a booth in the back, near the kitchen. There she proceeded to hide under the table, peeking out from between the legs of two women seated at the booth, one young and one middle aged. As they approached, Jan's full attention was held by the child, who had started a game of peek-a-boo with her. The seated women rose. "Cherie, Mrs. Folsom?" Sean asked. "Yes, I'm Cherie, you must be Mr. and Mrs. MacDowell. Welcome to Portland," the young woman replied. "This is Mrs. Doughty, one of our treasured Medical Foster Home Providers, and it looks like you've already met Mareena."

They shook hands all round, Jan interspersing peek-a-boo's between pleasantries. "Yes, their flight was on time. Yes, their hotel was adequate. Car rental had gone smoothly." The Oregon Social Worker was younger than Jan had expected. Close to Jan and Sean's age. Probably her first job out of college. It explained her enthusiasm and efficiency throughout their phone and mail correspondence. No burn out apparent yet. Pleasant features, long glossy hair and sensible attire. The Foster Mother too, was well-presented, comfortably-padded, motherly and warm. She cuddled a shyer girl on her lap. This dark haired child hugged her Foster Mother, burying her head in Mrs. Doughty's ample arm. Mareena, tiring of play, eventually climbed up too, nestling on Mrs. Doughty's lap, but remaining curious and watchful. Using her fingers to tuck in to the strawberry pancakes on the plate before her.

The greetings over, Jan and Sean slid onto the bench seat opposite, smiling at the bright faced child before them. She was nothing like they'd expected. She had the blonde hair and deep brown Bambi eyes found in the women of Sean's family. A lucky combination, enhanced by easily tanning skin that turned them into beach goddesses in the California sun. Sean's sisters were beauties, and this child most definitely belonged in his family. She had the spirit too. Adventurous, curious, playful and unafraid.

Jan's chest was fit to burst with joy. She hadn't expected to fall so immediately in love. They'd arrived braced for familial duty; in this Winter grayed, run down suburb, expecting to find a sickly, dull little foundling. Instead, a robust rosy cheeked, eager soul sat before them, examining them as curiously as they examined her.

Jan was delighted. A child with an adventurous and playful spirit. She and Sean had imagined a difficult year ahead. A year with their lives essentially on hold, as they nursed a child back to health then passed her back to the birth parents. Parents who Oregon Social Services assured them would get clean, to win re-unification with their four children. All of whom had been re-moved into foster care or adoption at Mareena's birth.

Except for the thin, lank, wispiness of her blonde hair, Maree-na bore no resemblance to her rangy addict father. None of his beaten demeanor, or shifty haunted gaze. In truth, it was the alert intelligence behind the child's direct gaze that captured Jan. There was no doubt now, they would give her a temporary home, be her family. Unite her with her older siblings, all whisked away from their parents when it became apparent their mother was still shooting heroin with a child in utero, and the father in jail.

It was hard to conceive that this lovely child had gone through withdrawals in a NICU before placement in Medical Foster Care. Mrs. Doughty was her second placement. Jan could not imagine what the child had been through. But it seemed she'd landed luckily, in competent, loving hands. The meeting lasted an hour. Jan and Sean, young themselves and just completing their final year at university, unaware that they were not asking the right questions. Ignorant to the possibility that serious questions needed to be asked. They trusted Sean's parents were caring for everyone's best interests. They owed his parents love and loyalty. Only one of his family members had gone astray, her mother-in-law's brother and only sibling. The rest on both sides, teachers, professors and professionals. Just one black sheep, Sean's Uncle. A heavy yoke for Sean's mother to bear. With resigned courage, Martha, Jan's mother-in-law, often quoted the African Proverb: "It takes a village to raise a child." Jan had agreed. Taking in the children was the right thing to do. It took a village, but first it took a family. This uplifting, family and community building idea resonated with Jan. Her career plans could be put on hold for one year. It was the least she and Sean could do for his parents. They had been so supportive of them as they began their married life.

Jan and Sean parted from the little group with hugs and kisses for the laughing child, caresses for the shy one. Mareena, the pretty vivacious toddler, returning to Mrs. Doughty's. Sean and Jan, driving back to their budget hotel, hoping to catch sleep before their early flight and drive back to San Bernardino, California. Cherie, the young Social Worker returning to the quiet Portland suburban home she shared with her husband. Satisfied that she'd achieved her goal of at least a temporary placement. Relieved in the knowledge that she was soon to cross one more child off her caseload.

Nairobi, 1969

BY ANNE MALCOLM

The reason for the visit is lost to memory, although after five decades the memory of our excitement remains. My father knew how to create a sense of adventure. He'd talked the trip up for weeks. As usual on travel days, we rose in darkness. The first horizontal line of morning light stretched over the eastern horizon as we climbed into the BMW. Four groggy kids shoehorned into the back seat. We moved silently so as not to disturb the neighbors, listening to the birdsong of the African morning, signifying all was well, no predators at large.

As my father drove, we left the small buildings and fruitful gardens of Machakos behind. The road passed small farms and bomas. Tiled, then corrugated roofs giving way to grass thatch. Rectilinear western buildings were replaced with round huts. The red-pink dawn spread to the east as the farmed areas surrounding our town petered out. By the time the sun peeked above the horizon, we'd entered the thorny shrublands of bush country, sweeping west from the Mua hills. Miles later, after turning onto the Mombasa road, the acacia-dotted grasslands of the East African plains opened before us, and the sun rose on paradise.

As an adult, my attention is still caught by morning or evening light glowing through tall waving grass. A sight more beautiful to me than any gaudy flower. It stops me in my tracks, and drops me into the flow state of the hunt. Because each of those childhood journeys, as we left the sanctuary of the town, was a hunt. Siblings vying for the reward of being the first to see a wild animal, usually a grazing herd of gazelles or a solitary male ostrich, but on rare occasions a giraffe or elephant herd in the far distance. We lived for our parent's approval, and a sighting brought their acclaim.

One hundred miles further on the Nairobi Mombasa road we

passed the turnoff to Amboseli at Athi River. The tarmac strip of a road, cut straight through the grassy plain. After the turnoff it showed more signs of wear. My father reduced his speed. Potholes became more frequent, the unshouldered road edge frayed. After miles without sign of human habitation or fellow travelers an occasional car would appear in the distance. Gradually the fencing of farms reappeared. Scattered huts, an occasional pedestrian walking purposefully along the vegetation-free dirt at the road edge. Car numbers gradually increased, signs, cardboard, and other human detritus signaled we were nearing the city. By now my father had slowed the car to a crawl dodging potholes, pedestrians, goats. Small businesses, clapboard shops, and street vendors began to line the road. People walking, bustling, trading on the dirt road verge. More people than we'd ever seen. The sun was now high in the sky, and the heat was building. We opened the windows. The unforgettable smell of Africa, cooking smoke, roasting maize, dust, animals and human sweat blew on warm winds into the car.

We entered the industrious communities of the outer city. The matatus appeared, presenting real hazards to drivers and pedestrians alike. They dodged into oncoming traffic to avoid potholes, screeched off the tarmac sending up clouds of dust as they picked up new fares. Baskets, colorful bundles, goats and chickens joining the people in the overflowing mini buses. Young men and boys riding the outer bumpers when the internal spaces were full.

We skirted the edge of Kibura. Concrete buildings and honking traffic began to replace the color and burgeoning life of the outer townships and slums. Exhaust fumes assaulted our nostrils and we closed the windows, choosing to sweat in the heat rather than breathe choking fumes. Makeshift street lights hanging on wires above intersections began to appear. Beggars risked their lives at intersections in hopes of kindness and handouts. Legless men on ingenious wheeled wood platforms scooted window to car window. Cracked dusty hands reaching towards drivers and passengers. White palmed, brown backed. Blind men, noseless women, children with flies in their eyes.

Satiated with our favorite soda, fizzy Fanta and the ginger biscuits Mom had baked for the journey, we children stared from the back seat in helpless horror. Dad pushed on doggedly through the noise and traffic. We climbed into the hills of the eastern city suburbs. Past the rolling green lawns and explosions of color in the flowering tropical trees of Uhuru Park. Past long razor wire topped walls hiding manicured estates. We turned through tall gates, past white-gloved guards into the shaded parking lot of the Norfolk Hotel. As our parents herded us onto the patio where iced coffee was served, and pristine washrooms beckoned with clean water flowing from the taps; we felt the disequilibrium that would return throughout our lives. We knew deep inside that something was very wrong.

minibeast

BY SHANNON MALLOY

this delicate tongue is sharp   and delicious
tapping on teeth   to make music and chaos

teeth tapping makes music   and in the chaos
we wrap ourselves around and become   each other

wrapped around each other we become   ourselves
and forget about parasites invading   our dreams

forget   about the parasites and invade   my dreams
before you've been sucked dry and eaten   alive

before you've been sucked alive   and eaten dry
I want to hold your breath   in my mouth

I want your hold,   your mouth,   to *be* your breath
and to taste every   moment   you spoke   your truth

I tasted your truth   the moment you spoke   and
your delicious   tongue   is delicate   and sharp

From Panic to Sandwich at 3 a.m.

by Shannon Malloy

3:01 a.m.:   the wave of dizzy and nausea plunges through
me from pinky toe to crown
third eye closes, the useless ones blur

3:03 a.m.:   sound muffles while the bell between my ears
strikes 3 times

3:04 a.m.:   bats flap their wings vicious in my belly
straight edges wave and tunnels close
around my corneas

3:13 a.m.:   warm velvet brushes my legs and arms
paws placed gently on my body…
the tunnels are behind me
the bats flew out of my navel
the bell fades back to static
4 eyes watch from the crook of my knee and the
cave of my chest
and now I can breathe as I have become their
peanut butter

shedding

by Shannon Malloy

inhale oxygen, exhale poison
open windows and slam doors
chew my cuticles, pick my nose, pet my dog, pet myself, piss
    myself and fight off predators

tap my foot, break my nails, hold my breath, count heart beats
    count sheep

shed my uterine lining and yank on strings, empty cups, not
    flush baby wipes down the toilet but

wipe my ass on the ass who cut me off on the empty road
rub smudges of eyeliner off my cheek, smudges of sex off my thigh,
    smudges of *me* off of
    others

taste my eyelashes, tickle nightmares
dance on hyacinth
write poetry on light waves
lick lollipops and swing on butterfly wings
I know I am human bc I'm singeing my eyebrows smoking one last
    cigarette, lighting my
    essence on fire

Cricket

BY MAE WAGNER MARINELLO

Due to overcrowding, the San Bernardino Animal Shelter was going to have to start euthanizing animals.

That was the news Gabrielle, my daughter, saw on Facebook–and it was tough news for both of us to take as we are animal lovers–especially dogs. My dog, Sophie, had died about two years ago—and I still missed her immensely. She had seen me through so much– good times and bad–which included the deaths of my husband, his youngest daughter, and my best friend of 59 years all within a span of two months, followed by a forced move.

I hadn't planned to get another dog, primarily due to my age and severe chronic pain, as well as living in a small space with no fenced yard. This meant that I would again need to walk a dog several times a day, should I get one—but Gabby and I were haunted by the Animal Shelter's message about euthanizing animals. Her family already had two good-sized dogs, plus one small dog and a menagerie of other animals, including a cat, cockatiel, rabbit, three goats and seven chickens. Thus, it would be up to me to reduce the dog population by one.

So, off to the animal shelter we went.

Let me tell you, a walk through the animal shelter is not for the faint of heart– unless you were somehow able to convince many others to adopt. It is heart-wrenching to see how many animals need a home. They bounce and pace round the cage they share with several others; they bark, and whine and their eyes plead with you to take them home. The San Bernardino Shelter even provided special incentives to try to ease overcrowding. There would be no charge for the animals—they would microchip it and have it spayed or neutered, if needed.

One cage held about six or seven young dogs who were obviously from the same litter. They were still medium size and so appealing; they had short, kind of a blondish-silver fur and their eyes were enchanting. Oh! I just knew those dogs would make wonderful pets and I would have adopted two of them in a heartbeat if only I had a proper home for them and if I were a few years younger.

When we had checked in at the front office, they told us to write down the cage number and the information provided about the dog if we found one we wanted and to bring that information to them. If it had been there less than a week, they held it in case an owner came looking for it; we were to return in one week at 11 a.m. and, if no one had claimed it, it would be mine. If we weren't there and someone else had put their name on the list, they could get the dog.

We came to the last aisle. It had cages on only one side, facing a grassy area. It was beginning to look like I wasn't going to find a dog for me. I didn't know if I felt relief or disappointment.

There were only about three cages left.

And there she was.

She looked like a smaller version of Sophie as she cowered in a front corner of Cage #A548749. The intake date was August 23, 2022, and the available date was August 30, 2022. The description of her was "fearful" and, "This dog is a spayed female, white, West Highland, 2yr."

She had only been there one day! And the description could not have been any better—except for the fearful part—but I knew that would change when she settled into her new home just as Sophie had. I wanted a female; she was already spayed and they guessed her to be a West Highland terrier. (She must have come from a loving home as she was spayed. I felt sorry for whomever had somehow lost her.)

We were so excited! We returned to the front office and put my name—the first—on the list for the dog the shelter folks had named Petra. We were to return in a week at 11 a.m., my name would be called and, if no owner had claimed her, she would be mine. Or I would be hers, whichever the case may be.

A week later, we were there to adopt our treasure. There was also a woman and her high-school age son there to claim their chosen dog. I was almost as excited for them as I was for myself for they had chosen one from the litter that Gabby and I had found so appealing. I told them they really needed to adopt two of them! I have wondered if they did return for another; the one they got would be very lonely for its siblings.

Every single member of the staff at the shelter had been a pleasure to deal with and the two young ladies who appeared, ready to microchip "Petra" were no exception. They were joyful and efficient. I couldn't believe I had shown up without a collar or leash! I had donated almost all of Sophie's things to the Redlands Animal Shelter. (I kept two of her favorite toys.) No collar? No leash? No problem! The two young ladies managed to supply those necessary items, too.

I couldn't believe I was walking out of the shelter with a new dog! On the way home, we stopped at a pet store. I bought a toy, food and dog crate. I had never used a crate for any of my dogs in the past.

I decided to re-name my new companion; I had done the same to Sophie. Our family dog during my childhood was named Cricket and this seemed like a good name for this joyful little creature! And so, Cricket she became! And oh! What joy Cricket has brought, not just to me but to many others as well.

I would encourage anyone who is even remotely thinking of getting a pet—don't buy, please adopt! Every dog I have ever had, with the exception of one more than 60 years ago, including Sophie, has been a rescue.

Three Red Roses

BY ELISSE MARTINEZ

Eliud Martínez was eight years old when a newspaper reporter in Austin spotted him hunched over a picnic table, pencil and paper in hand. It was 1943. There was a war on. The little boy, who eventually became my husband, was drawing soldiers and tanks. He learned to draw by copying from Superman comic books.

Estroberto and María, Eliud's parents, framed the story and hung it on the kitchen wall. This would not be the last time someone became smitten by his talent.

Eliud was bilingual at an early age. His father taught him to read and write in Spanish using the daily Spanish newspaper. During the 1940s speaking Spanish at school was discouraged: students caught speaking Spanish on the playground had their hands slapped with a ruler!

His art talent was promoted by his teachers who called him *novio*, "sweetheart." He continued to draw all through school and was chosen to attend the one high school in Austin for college-oriented students, while his peers from his barrio went to the vocational school to learn a trade. This was an emotional, life-changing transition for Eliud.

In his junior year a kind teacher, Miss Greenley, called him "Van Gogh." She would catch him drawing in class and say with a heavy Southern drawl, "We all admire your art talent, but this is an *English class*." He loved to quote her in later years.

He attended the University of Texas as a Fine Arts major on the GI Bill after serving as a Marine during the Korean war. College was held in such high regard in his family that he dressed in a suit and tie the first week of class. Eventually he realized the art students were wearing T-shirts and jeans to class.

The first time I ever saw Eliud's art was the first time I met him. The young artist was wearing a black T-shirt and blue jeans with a wide black leather belt. I walked into his art show at a small gallery in the village that was showing his surrealist oil paintings. The screaming reds and dynamic blues captivated me. The young artist captivated me, too.

I later learned that as early as grade school Eliud's name became "Elin," perhaps because the name Eliud was unfamiliar, and even his family started calling him Elin. He didn't use Eliud until one professor questioned him about his name. After some research he and the professor discovered his name was Eliud, which in Hebrew means "Hand of God."

Years later, on a trip to the Sistine Chapel in the Vatican, as Eliud and I stretched our necks to see Michaelangelo's fresco on that high ceiling, we were moved with emotion to find the letters of the Biblical name spelled out: E-L-I-U-D. Chills went down my spine.

Eliud always kept up his love of art, sketching and painting. When he began to travel more, he found carrying art supplies challenging. He began to write short stories and to keep a daily journal. Later he became a professor of creative writing, literature and Chicano studies. At home a huge wooden easel stood like a sentry in the garage where he would often paint.

Too soon the years passed. For Eliud, old age also came with Parkinson's disease, and his art talent was diminished by his physical disabilities.

On my birthday, Eliud would always bring me my favorite flowers, a dozen red roses. The last year of his life on my birthday he asked his caregiver, María, to buy a dozen red roses. She put them in a lovely crystal vase. I took out three red roses and put them in a small vase by Eliud's dinner plate.

After dinner he asked for his whiteboard and markers, which he used to sketch and would play games with me, like tic-tac-toe and hangman. With great effort he lifted the red marker and drew three red roses, then a green maker for leaves and stems, and finally a black marker, with slow deliberate moves, to draw a vase around them. He even added his signature.

It brought tears to my eyes to watch his laborious efforts. The drawing, although primitive, was so touching. I took a photo and will cherish this memento of a great artist and his enduring love.

"Oh Sister"

BY ELISSE MARTINEZ

January 21, 2023

"Oh Sister, oh Sister," was the call to come outside and play during my young years in Buffalo, New York. My name is Elisse, but my brother, Brian, 3 years my senior, always called me "Sister." It caught on with friends and family.

Picture me, a small seven-year-old with a dark blonde bob-style haircut and big blue eyes. "A shayna maidel," *pretty girl*, translated from Yiddish, was how my Russian grandparents described me. I preferred to be a tomboy.

The children on my block played outside all day on non-school days. It was a carefree, innocent childhood. Our bodies were active all day, riding scooters, bikes, roller skating, playing ball, or having races. We also liked to dig for worms and watch the ant colonies. We did not have technology or social media to distract our growing brains. Our imagination was engaged constantly, inventing new games and relating to nature.

"Kinder require *naches* (fun), not *sores* (troubles)," my grandpa would say.

On one crisp October day, with leaves on the oak trees turning yellow and orange under a clear blue sky, I set off to play. I wore a red plaid flannel shirt and blue Levi dungarees with big belt loops. Most important were the sturdy Buster Brown Oxfords on my feet. *Run like a cheetah*, I thought, *and catch up with my brother*.

The block we lived on, Villa Avenue, had four boys, but no girls as yet. The boys decided to have a running race on this beautiful fall day, and the winner would get a dime. Each boy put in two pennies. The race track covered four back yards with two chain link fences to jump. Mike yelled, "On your mark, Get Set, Get

Ready, Go!" We all ran. I was fast for my age, but of course they were much faster and taller. It would be great to get a dime for a comic book or my favorite candy, Mallo Cups, chocolate covered creamy coconut. We all jumped over one fence and ran so fast our leg muscles were overworked. All the boys were way ahead. By the time I reached the last yard I was out of breath and could not get over the fence. I ended up hanging by my Levi belt loop upside down on the fence. I screamed and yelled, "Help!"

By chance, my Grandpa Ray was visiting my mom, Mollie. He lived a mile away and liked to walk to our house and bring fresh fruits and vegetables from the Farmer's Market. "Oy gevalt, Mollie, there is a little girl hanging upside down on the fence in the next yard!" Mollie looked out the window and screamed, "Oy, vey, it's Sister!" Grandpa ran across the grass and lifted me carefully off the chain link fence and carried me home. I cried all the way.

It was warm and inviting in our kitchen; bright shiny red apples were on the table. Mom cut one up for me. It was juicy and delicious. I was starting to feel better.

What a surprise when Grandpa Ray said, "Sister, you were so brave, you deserve a dime!" Elated, I gave him a big hug.

So Many Unanswered Questions

by Rose Y. Monge

It happens regularly to me. I begin writing a new memoir with a single focus. Suddenly, I'm spiraling into a deep emotional vortex replete with bittersweet collateral memories. This is one of the stories. My plan is to write about my only grandparent and my namesake-Nana Rosa. However, thinking about her takes me to my cultural background, the possible origin of my surname and regrets of not having a relationship with my extended Monge family. I have so many unanswered questions!

I hear heartfelt stories about grandparents from my schoolmates. They describe loving celebrations, vacations and heartfelt memories with plenty of hugs. I'm a tad envious as Nana Rosa, Dad's mom is my only grandparent. My paternal grandfather, Tata Antonio died when I'm a toddler and I have no memory of him. Mom is an orphan at an early age.

Growing up and even into my adulthood, I know little about her. A few tidbits of information surfaces haphazardly over the years. Dad mentions that she grew up in Sonora, Mexico-the land of the indigenous tribe, the Yaquis.

The Yaqui connection intrigues me so I go to the Internet. I learn that the "Yaquis endure centuries of pain and suffering protecting their native land. It's notable that the Yaquis are the only indigenous tribe not subjugated by the Spanish conquistadores." The tribe numbers around 30,000 at its height living peacefully in northern Mexico.

"At the turn of the century, the Mexican government offers the land to foreign investors in hopes of colonizing the sparse, fertile northern states. It is estimated that the 8,000 to 15,000 Yaquis who resisted were rounded up; imprisoned; or sold as slaves from 1904-1909. Many would die within the first year due to the climate and the inhuman working conditions. Some went into hiding or fled to Arizona. The bloody civil war raged for years. And each time, the government was met with Yaqui resistance. In 1939, President Cardenas, granted the Yaqui tribe official recognition and title to their land." (*Yaqui: A Short History* by Edith te Wechel, Las Culuras.com)

I can only imagine the perspective my Nana has during this time period as she was born in 1898. How did her family survive the civil war that rages in their homeland during those turbulent times? I will never know.

Nana marries Antonio Monge at 16 years old. I wonder when, where and how my grandparents meet. How he ends in Agua Prieta, my birthplace is another mystery. Eventually, Nana has eight children: five sons and three daughters. According to Dad, our Tata is a humble and hardworking man. He owns a small family milpa where he grows seasonal produce. In the winter, he sells firewood for the wood burning stoves. Dad's brothers help Tata in the milpa before moving away from Agua Prieta to establish their own families. Dad is the last of the siblings to work on the family farm.

Upon Tata's death, Nana immigrates to California in the Imperial Valley and settles in El Centro. At the time, she still has three children living with her. Dad's other siblings also leave Mexico and settle close to Nana's with the exception of two siblings who stay in Mexico near the California/Mexico border. Over the years, we visit our aunts and uncles but never forge a strong relationship. I regret not having the opportunity to have a relationship with my cousins.

In the early 1950's, Dad realizes that the milpa can no longer be able to provide a viable source of income for the family so he begins the extensive paperwork to leave Mexico. Because he's bringing the entire family, it will take years to complete. We arrive in the Riverside area in the late 1950's. During the first 10 years, we live in the unincorporated area of Etiwanda. The vineyard owners provide us abandoned homes in exchange for tending the fields. The family joins the migrant circuit in the summers since Dad's income barely covers feeding our large family that includes 10 children by 1961. Dad is able to buy a home in 1964 in Rubidoux. Finally, our migrant experience is over.

Dad tries to keep in touch with Nana whenever he can or when we're not working. He loads us up in his trusty Ford station wagon and drives to El Centro. Our visits are brief, just a few hours. The house is small with only 3 rooms with a smelly outhouse nearby. Mom usually brings food to prepare a meal in the tiny kitchen. I don't enjoy being there as I feel uncomfortable sitting quietly so as not to interrupt the adults. Mom tells us not to touch anything.

Dad's youngest brother, Uncle Joe whom we call "Chuy," lives with her. He is just a few years older than my oldest sister, Trini. He's sullen and morose, hardly speaking to us. Dad tells us he worries about him since he stays out late with friends, and isn't doing well in school. Nana decides to move to Ontario possibly to give Chuy an opportunity to change his behavior. Her house is close to our abandoned homes in Etiwanda. Upon high school graduation, Chuy joins the Army. The military becomes his career and we lose contact with him. I see him at Nana's funeral in 1979, at Dad's service in 1994, and Mom's in 2011. He becomes another stranger to the Monge family.

In retrospect, Nana is so unlike my dad as he's so easy going and patient with us. I hear her chastising Mom for her parenting but Mom keeps her silence out of respect. It's ironic that Mom's only role model for parenting is our Nana. I don't recall a time when I hear her laugh. Nana's criticisms also include Dad. She often compares him unfavorably to his other siblings particularly with Uncle Manuel, the eldest son. Dad brushes off the criticisms and copes patiently with her snubs.

I'm not sure what Uncle Manuel does for a living but he's fond of wearing a white shirt and tie. My Uncle, rest his soul, puts on airs and often criticizes Dad as well. Nobody compares to him as Nana frequently reminds us: *Look at your uncle, doesn't he look handsome in his suit and tie? His house is so big and beautiful. Have you seen it?*

Somehow, Uncle Manuel convinces Nana to convert from the Catholic faith to the Jehovah's Witness. Several aunts and uncles follow suit. Mom and Dad refuse to do so and our family is ostracized. Visits now become almost non-existent.

Why doesn't our Nana show more affection towards us? Her gentle embrace and words would have meant the world to me. I love and respect her for being Dad's mother but her death in 1979 leaves me with many unanswered questions.

Another question emerges as I write this story. What is the origin of my surname? It's not a common Hispanic name. From the history of Mexico, I learn that France tries to occupy Mexico twice in the 1830'and the 1860's. Both attempts are unsuccessful. Their defeat in Puebla is commemorated as Cinco de Mayo in the United States embraced by youth of Mexican heritage involved in the civil rights movement. Dad never likes the label "Chicano." The official Mexico's Independence Day is September 16 and celebrated in Mexico but it's hardly embraced in the United States.

Is there some French blood in the Monge lineage? Maybe. There's a possibility that Tata's ancestors might have been French due to our last name. How many soldiers stayed in Mexico after the Franco-Mexican Wars? Over the years, it delights me whenever I meet Monges from many countries not limited to Central and South America.

A few years ago, my younger sister, Sally and her family went to France. She tells me that the 5th "arrondissement" (district) in Paris was named for Gaspard Monge. His biography mentions that he was born on May 9, 1746 and died on July 28, 1818. He is considered the founder of differential geometry. The 5th arrondissement is close to the Latin Quarter. According to my sister Sally, the "Place Monge" or the Monge Plaza in Paris is thriving with upscale hotels, restaurants, shops and markets. Who knew that there would be a Monge presence in Paris?

Over the years and after my parents' passing, my siblings and I often speak about "growing up" Monge. Five of us are born in Mexico and the other five in California. We have many "what ifs" about our grandparents and parents' lives that had an impact on all of us. What if our family had stayed in Mexico? What if our Tata had been part of our life? What if Mom had been raised by her parents? What if Nana would have been loving like our Dad? The list goes on and on.

As an aside, I found a website recently that mentions the Yaqui tribe. In Tucson, Arizona, the Pascua Yaqui Tribe is the only federally recognized Yaqui tribe in the USA and has more than 13,000 member citizens. The family hopes to explore more of our family roots. Maybe some answers may emerge. Or perhaps new questions may arise.

Insectum Digestum

BY MAURY MORTENSEN

Amuse-bouche, appetizer, breakfast, lunch or dinner,
Any insect prepared with style and a fancy sauce is a winner.
Insect cookery and consumption is all the rage,
This list of bug treats may just fill a page.

Starters may be Moths on melon balls with toast points,
Or near dead Mantis or Termites with moving joints.
Ground Crickets, Scorpions, Locusts and Grasshoppers,
Make tasty crunchies for ice cream sundae toppers.

A nice Gnat-a-tuille, or some steamed Flies in your soup,
Creamed Katydid and Centipede makes a foamy green goop.
A refreshing Stinger with crème de menthe and a fine brandy,
With pureed Bee, Wasp or Hornet, a cocktail nicer than candy.

Or, a tasty entrée favorite of sautéed Mice, rice and lice.
For dessert, a Weevil Waffle with Chocolate Chip Aphids, so nice.
Ground Butterflies and Mayflies with sour cream, makes a great dip,
For T.V. treats, I like Cheetos Mosquitos and Dragonfly Chips.

A food truck might exclusively offer a selection of Roaches.
German, Oriental, Brown Banded and Suri nan: truly Roach Coaches.
Sauteed or simmered, smoked, toasted or in a bake,
Whole or in pieces, crushed, rendered or infused into a cake.

When shopping in your yard for these protein rich little critters,
I would avoid going barefoot; oh look over there, it's a Mayfly fritter.
The choices are endless, your grocery your garden,
Using insects in your cooking is even endorsed by Ina Garten.

Bug Appetite

My Life in Summers

by Barbara Mortensen

I was asked a simple question: What do you plan to do for the summer? And, I was to answer the question in writing. Ah, so why then was this such a difficult piece for me to write?

Maybe because it conjures up all kinds of memories, going all the way back to my very early childhood when life and summers seemed so simple.

Maybe because when I was six years old, swimming in the ocean with my friends came with the admonishment from all of our parents: "if you drown don't come home because I will kill you!" This cry still resonates in my ear.

Maybe because digging for clams with adult strangers never came with the thought that the strangers would hurt me, but with the knowledge that I wasn't supposed to bring the clams home or eat them because they weren't kosher!

Maybe because my first crush was a little six-year-old boy whose parents wouldn't let me play with him because I was Jewish and I didn't understand why that mattered!

Maybe because Christmas was in December, and it was always cold and almost always snowy until I spent Christmases in South America and in the Caribbean and in Africa and in Australia when Christmas was in the summertime and I surprisingly pined for the cold beauty of a Christmas winter.

Maybe because it is an almost lost remembrance of our family trying to get away from the bitter cold of winter by chasing summer all the way down the Florida coast so that we could bask in the warmth of the southern Atlantic Ocean.

Maybe because the car trip south meant that we had to encounter water fountains and bathrooms and gas pumps and restaurants designated for whites only! And my parents had to explain why those signs were there.

Maybe because once I knew and understood, the trip south became sad because none of this made any sense to me.

Maybe because I now live in the desert where it is almost always summer and what I will do during the summer is what I will, for the most part, do in the winter.

Maybe because since COVID, going away in the summer isn't as easy or exciting as it used to be: crowded planes, crowded airports, expensive gas, expensive hotels, expensive babysitters and boarding for my treasured animals.

Maybe because I am too old to be as bold as I was and live up to my dreams or......

Maybe because almost all of my summer dreams have come true and now I am content to stay home in the summer and enjoy my home and one of the many pools in my country club and maybe visit with friends whom I adore and who seem to adore me.

Maybe because now that it is summer, a new milestone has passed: a new rocket to space was launched without me in it! I am too old and not rich enough to have been one of the selected passengers.

Maybe because almost all of the wishes of my life have come to pass except this one dream of mine: to fly into space. So, while I swim and sun and relax, I will continue to dream of what could have been my perfect summer: to be launched into space for the ride and the summer of my lifetime!!!!!

My Father

BY BARBARA MORTENSEN

I have written about me, I have written about my mother, I have written about my aunt, my friends, about other relationships I have had. But, until now, I have never written just about my father. Why?

I think it is because I am still angry with him for dying and dying while suffering with senile dementia. Yes, this gloriously brilliant man with an unbelievably great mind died not knowing who he was nor recognizing who we, his family, were.

It could be that I am angry with him for not being the traditional version of a loving father.

You see, my father was not affectionate. He wasn't a hugger, nor an embracer, nor a kisser.

Not to his children, not to his wife, not to any of his family. It was only when I became an adult and I teased him into hugging and embracing me so frequently that it finally became a habit for him to do so whenever he saw me.

As I learned later in life, his lack of demonstrative affection wasn't because he didn't care about us, but because of his upbringing: he was raised to believe it wasn't manly to show affection. The first and only time I saw him cry was at the funeral Mass of one of his closest friends.

It could be that my anger was displaced: my anger should have been with his parents and not with my father.

But, how can I be angry with a grandfather I never met except through hearsay, photos and artwork, who actually saved my father's life? You see, my father was born in Poland, to a well to do very well-known educated family of artists and educators, engineers and doctors. Life should have been easy for my father, but it wasn't: because during that era Germany occupied Poland and the German army was going to conscript my fifteen-year-old father into the army. This meant almost certain death for him. So, my grandfather left his wife and three younger children and brought my father to the United States where, whatever life would be, at least my father would be alive!

My father who had been destined to become an engineer or a mathematician or an artist, like his father before him, was denied these choices because first, he had to learn English and then at fifteen years old find a way to earn money to survive in the United States. He did survive to be ninety-four, never wanted for anything, never complained. You see, in spite of such a difficult start in life, he was so bright, he got his education; and we, his children not only got educated but lived what would be called the "good life" because of him.

My father could do anything. He could build anything. He could design anything. He could fix anything. He could draw anything. I know that I am still angry with him because I don't have enough of his incredible paintings. I don't have any of his doodles that were drawn on a paper napkin every evening at dinner time. What a lovely little book they would have made!

My father thought and expressed his thoughts on paper. There wasn't a mathematical problem he couldn't solve. I never had a tailor because my father always figured out how to make something fit me. His first job was sewing slipcovers and drapes for an interior design firm. He taught me how to sew. I still have his famous old Singer sewing machine.

He became a renowned interior designer in NYC. Many of his clients were the Mafia ladies of New York. He almost never met the husbands but the wives were enchanted by the way he decorated their mansions.

My father loved music, particularly symphonic music and most particularly Beethoven. Sometimes when we were driving with the car radio blasting, my mother would have to admonish my father to stop conducting, put his hands back on the wheel and to drive before he got us all killed!

My father loved to travel and instilled me with the travel bug. We drove almost everywhere in the United States. The one place he refused to visit was Europe. His comment was always "I have already been there and saw enough." He came to visit me in every country I ever lived except, he was true to himself: he never visited me when I lived in Europe.

My father loved the movies and the theater. He started taking me with him to all the late night movies when I was two years old. There is an era of movies I shouldn't really know about, but of which I am an expert. I loved the movies my father took me to and I never forgot those late night evenings with him nor the movies we saw together.

He loved the United States. He considered Thanksgiving to be his birthday because he said he became a naturalized American citizen on Thanksgiving Day. In his honor, on Thanksgiving, I always make a big celebratory dinner.

I really adored my father but I also had massive arguments with him because he was very strong-willed and stubborn. I inherited that stubborn nature from him. He was the disciplinarian in the house and as children; he spanked us for untoward deeds. I guess this is what he thought it took to make a good father. However, if there was a problem to be solved, if you were ill, if the dog was ill, if there was something wrong, he was the first one to be at your side comforting you in his own inimical style.

My father was a great athlete and maintained his weight and physique for all of his life without ever trying to do so even though I don't think he ever had a meal that didn't have some form of potato in it. Even when there was nothing left in his head, his body, at ninety-four years old was as firm and solid and athletic and strong as a much much younger man. I think I am still angry with him because I would rather have had his mind survive the ravages of age than to have his body survive in such good shape. He was a beautiful corpse.

My father was liberal in his politics and encouraged us to believe in freedom and democracy. He was a leader and was honored by being president of his various organizations and associations.

He was a very good storyteller, well loved by his friends, some of whom he still knew from Poland. His friends were all doctors, lawyers, engineers, philosophers. A chance meeting led to a very long and fond friendship with the great actor Louis Jordan. People clung to him for his talent and intellect and mostly for his honesty and wisdom. He never discouraged us from challenges. He was an avid reader and dinner time at our house encouraged the liveliest if not heated discussions.

I think his greatest joy was moving to California. He loved the Wild West and everything western. To this day, when I drive through HWY 79 in California now, a modern HWY, I can remember his delight when we would drive through what was then just a narrow mountain pass and he could envision the cowboys and Indians hiding behind the enormous boulders. I can remember when he drove up to Utah. I think he loved St. George and the landscape in Utah better than any other place he had ever been. Sadly, there are no drawings or paintings of his frequent visits to Utah.

I believe that in his own way he quietly suffered because in the era in which he lived, it became common to change your surname so you wouldn't be considered either a communist or to be Jewish and be discriminated against: think McCarthy era. Many in our family did change their names. My father never did. He was proud of his origins and his name and he never believed in hiding who you were. But he hated being called a "Pollock" and its derogatory intentions.

Sometimes we did with much less so that my father could support those family members or friends who came from oppressive countries or concentration camps so that they could get a start in their new lives in the United States. In his lifetime he was the sole support not only of my family: my mother, brother and me, but also for his older sister and her family of four and his younger brother and his family of four. I was often angry with him because sometimes he didn't give me what I thought was enough of my allowance. I thought he was too busy taking care of everyone else but us, his immediate family.

But the things I can't be angry with him for is the value system he instilled in me; of not to be afraid to speak up, to work for the betterment of our society, to be inquisitive, to read, to learn, to care and most of all to love music and art and to make music and art an integral part of my live. He always said, "Challenge yourself, you don't know what will come of the challenge but it will at least have been interesting." Unfortunately, his great artistic talent wasn't passed on to me! I don't draw very well but at least what he passed on to me was a love of art and a great eye for recognizing good art. I am a museum and gallery hound because of him.

Religion was a different story. My father's family were mainly Jewish, but Jewish or not, they all were held in esteem by my father for their deeds and not their religion. Since he was not a practicing Jew, I had to come by my religious knowledge and caring for my religion late in my own lifetime without the guidance of my father.

I am angry with him because he was still the best person I knew of to talk to and dialogue with about anything and everything. But, in retrospect, I think I am angry at the wrong people. Maybe I should be angry with myself for not retaining more of what I know about my father and his wisdom. He, to my mind, was and is still the most intelligent, well read and inquisitive person I have ever met in my life. I am most angry with him because he is not here with me now!

Mobsters and Zombie Cocktails: My Adventure Through Tikidom

BY CINDI NEISINGER

Alright, folks, brace yourselves for a wild ride through my Tiki-filled adventure! Let's set the scene first... *"Alexa, play Hawaiian music."*

It all began when I stumbled upon a rare, gold-embossed red leather book in my mother's backyard shed. Imagine my surprise when I cracked it open and discovered a treasure trove of 1940s business documents from none other than Don the Beachcomber, Inc. in Chicago. But here's the thing – some of these documents had mob signatures! You can guess what happened next; curiosity grabbed me by the MuuMuu dress. I couldn't Google it fast enough! Who was the mastermind behind this treasure trove, and who was pulling the strings at Don the Beachcomber, Inc.?

Naturally, I dove headfirst into the online abyss, determined to unearth the truth. That book felt like a diary, detailing the birth of the Don the Beachcomber restaurant in Chicago. The fact is a restaurant chain with a man's name was run by a woman. The book ended up in Riverside, California, my town. It's a plot twist deserving of its own episode on the U*nsolved Mysteries* TV series.

My writing journey whisked me away on a whirlwind tour of research and timelines. My initial plan was to craft a creative non-fiction novel around the enigmatic figure, Sunny Sund, the genius behind the iconic Don the Beachcomber Restaurants in Hollywood, Chicago, and Palm Springs. But hold on to your leis, my initial online searches led to a big fat zero. No Wikipedia page, nada! It was like she was a phantom in the world of Tiki. Unknown.

But destiny had other plans in store for me. Enter Karen Sund, Sunny's daughter, who waltzed onto the scene like a literary muse.

Well, I texted her after I found her name online. I had heard rumors of Sunny having a daughter, and I was grateful when I finally tracked her down—and she didn't hang up on me. Instead of my original plan, Karen and I embarked on an epic journey to complete her forty-year-old manuscript—a manuscript chronicling the untold story of her mother's life.

Karen told me many stories about the Hollywood stars in her and her mother's life. Major ones: Sinatra, her god-mother Mary Pickford, and even Tarzan, otherwise known as Johnny Weissmuller who taught her how to swim. Sunny was a brilliant restaurateur and business woman that had dealings with the Chicago outfit, which came with its challenges. Ironically, a restaurant famous for its rum rhapsodies was also the catalyst of her battle with alcoholism. Still, Sunny had a legacy that deserved the spotlight. We decided to write her biography/memoir. A woman in a man's world, who succeeded beyond her wildest dreams.

Our collaboration began with me as Karen's Latina ghostwriter, but my role evolved over time. I became her co-writer, after surprising her with my research from before she was born. I showed her stories written in historical books, newspapers and magazines. Sunny was a star in her own right. The two-year journey with Karen (three years for me) was like a rollercoaster of writing. There were moments when we wanted to fire each other, "You're Fired!" "NO! I quit!" But our partnership hit a hard stop when Karen received a breast cancer diagnosis. Instead of parting ways, it brought us closer, more determined than ever to put her book in one hand and a Mai Tai in the other. Our professional relationship morphed into an unbreakable friendship. There have been sleepovers, and very few days we don't text something… if only a cute emoji. But, fuck cancer!

This quest turned me into a Tiki aficionada, and I started seeing tropical drinks with mint sprigs, fruit, and cocktail umbrellas in a whole new light. What I once considered kitsch became an integral part of the vibrant and immersive Tiki culture. It's escapism at its finest, my friends!

Shoutout to all my mentors who allowed me to crash their Tiki parties (you know, for research). At the top of the list, a heartfelt thanks to Tim "Swanky" Glazner, whose forthcoming book *Searching for Don the Beachcomber* is scheduled to be published in 2025. Another shout out to the producers behind the documentary–YES! A documentary is on the horizon, "The Donn of Tiki," a Surf Monkey Production. Scheduled for release in 2025. You don't want to miss Karen's interview. And don't blink… because I'm an animated background character. Hint: I'm dancing, in a party clip, wearing large black frame glasses and black/white hair. Cruella-ish.

Now, fast forward to today. Tiki culture is experiencing a revival, with documentaries, new books, events and venues popping up across the United States and around the globe. The brand name was purchased by a restaurant corporation that has plans to expand across the United States. In Sunny's honor they placed a drink on their menu, called Sunakora. It was created by her first husband Donn Beach for her to enjoy as she ran the business in Hollywood, Chicago and Palm Springs.

And there you have it, my epic Hollywood and Tiki-infused adventure with Karen Sund. A book we wrote filled with intrigue, original cocktail recipes, historical images, and—Wait! Did I tell you about the time Harpo Marx whistled a song to Karen at the Palm Springs Don the Beachcomber? It's all in our book. *Sunny Sund: The Woman Behind Don the Beachcomber, Inc. A Hollywood Story.*

In a world dominated by constant and unsettling "Breaking News," the whimsical escapism offered by Donn and Sunny's legacy and the Don the Beachcomber Brand is more welcome than ever.

But wait, folks! Let's not break the Tiki ambiance. Mahalo!

Berry Pie

by Deborah Nevárez-Vivolo

We left for the fancy Music Center in Downtown LA after a lunch of tacos de peanut butter or tuna sandwiches (Grandma Sarah let us choose), and we all piled into Grandpa Shorty's chocolate-brown Dodge Dart. When we got there, me and my little brother Damien liked walking by all the fountains outside (I saw some people toss pennies into the water for good luck) and climbing a crystal staircase to our bouncy velvet seats! But why did we see this stupid play about a boy named Oliver, with a bunch of white kids singing and jumping up and down? Boor-ing!!! What's an Artful Dodger?

Since the bathroom lines were long after the play, Mom told us to "hold it" until later, only now we are not back at Grandma's. Grandpa Shorty drove us on the Pomona freeway past East L.A. towards home in South San Gabriel (where we hear a rooster crow in the morning), then got off near a golf course named after a cannon. The sky is now dark, inky blue and I see no stars. Only in Big Bear with the Cub Scouts do me and Damien see stars.

I pulled up the black button on the squeaky car door. We pile out onto Lucky's parking lot, the nearest "good" supermarket to Grandma's house. Not like La Quebradita with the smashed cans for sale. "Hey, stop pushing!" The streetlights hum above us. Damien is right, they kinda look like War of the Worlds alien heads. Damien doesn't like his name. He gets teased at school. Kids think he's the Omen. Sometimes he acts like a diablo Mom says.

I look up at the yellow and red Denny's sign. It glows. "Wait, we are going to Denny's? We NEVER go here! There's food at Grandma's," I mumble to myself. I hide the limp from the tight, plastic Heidi shoes Mom picked out of the Zody's bin for me, by kinda walking real slow, then tiptoeing. "These are fancy, Deb.

You could wear them for Easter." They are caca brown, shiny, plastic with black shoelaces, a green ribbon with tiny pink flowers sewn on the front. I hate them! They squeak. They already have scuff marks. Now my pinky toes and heels are sore. "You will break them in. You get what you get," she says.

I pull the Salvation Army sweater sleeves past my fingers. It's cold. A "late night, early morning" cold, like Dr. George, the TV weatherman says. "Qué frío!" I wish I had my puffy nylon jacket with the "Eskimo" hood. If I had it, I could hide my head, give myself a fluffy hug. Shrink to Thumbelina size. Poof. I want to go home to Mooney Drive. I think of my old room, my books from San Marino yard sales, my rock collection under the bed, and the mouse that hid there until Mom chased him out (hope she didn't smash the little guy, he looked like a baby). My own bed, night light, my record player, and Sparky outside on the porch make me smile, but they are gone. Dad let me take only what I could carry in my hands. "Don't cry," she said. Why can't we have a normal Mom and Dad?

My sweater cannot hide the gurgly sounds of my stomach, plus I gotta go! So does Damien! Mom is ahead of us with the primos, Auntie Pina, Uncle Edward, Grandma Sarah, and Grandpa Shorty. Then she turns around and gets me by the arm until I feel her uñas. "What I do wrong!?" My heart goes thump, thump like in a Bugs Bunny cartoon. She gives us "el ojo," the stink eye. "Chavalo and Miss Prissy: Don't order anything. You both get hot chocolate. That's it." We nod. I'm blinking cause maybe Mom's gonna give me a guantada with her hand, like the last time with her chancla from across the living room, that left a red mark. I get hot and embarrassed and want to disappear. Poof. Auntie Betty says Mom spits nails. I don't know what that is. Maybe it's our fault or Dad's that she eats nails. Damien ate glass marbles once.

We all smash into a long tan booth near the front window. The plastic flowers behind us poke our heads. My primos got French fries!!! Oh man, the fat, salty kind!! The hot chocolate is taking a long time! It comes hot and Swiss Miss cocoa sweet with Redi-Whip on top. Finally! But then the nice lady puts a piece of berry pie in front of me. It's purple like blackberries from Grandma Sarah's garden. Like Smucker's jam. This is a mistake! I'm gonna get it! I don't pick up the fork. I stare down at the fake wood tabletop and bite my lip hard. I wanna disappear. Poof.

My Uncle Edward stares at me behind his dark glasses at the end of the booth. He's rich! He's got a cool jet-black Challenger. Like Steve McQueen's movie car, you know? Very cherry, Dad would say. Uncle Edward plays tennis, is a lawyer like Perry Mason, and has a key to the Playboy Club, whatever that is. Why does he wear sunglasses at night? Mom doesn't like Uncle Edward, her older brother. She acts like he went poof! My uncle bends over the table and flicks the edge of my plastic plate like he does when he smokes cigarettes. "Go ahead. I bought it for you."

Airport Encounter

by Deborah Nevárez-Vivolo

"We know you have choices when you fly. Thank you for choosing Southwest Airlines. Welcome to San Jose." From my window seat, golden hills dotted with black oaks surrounding Mt. Hamilton, set against a turquoise sky, greeted my eyes. The Mammas and the Papas sang "California Dreamin'" in unison like an earworm on repeat; I did not mind at all. I was in a great mood because my dreams were coming true. The seat belt sign was turned off. As part of the UCLA Chicano Studies undergrad entourage, I collected my duffle and followed Tere, Connie, Peter, and post-doc Nestor out of the plane and up the ramp. The airport lobby was awash in sunlight streaming through its skylights, painting the rows of caramel-colored seats filling the gateways.

"Stanford here we come! Dios mío! Can you believe it, Tere?" "Look guys, we're on a tight schedule. Once we arrive on campus, there will be just enough time to unpack, before the welcome dinner at their faculty club, so don't be late, me entiendes?" Nestor acted like a self-assigned paternal figure and less a graduate student that day. Fine, cool. Whatever. Nothing is going to bug me today. I was a blend of nervous energy, hope, excitement. As one of the chosen few to study public policy for a semester under their world-class instructors, this would be an excellent foundation for graduate school. After last summer's LBJ fellowship in DC, this was also a fantastic precursor to my final year at UCLA. *The world is my oyster. What could go wrong?* I blissfully thought. *Just ace senior year. Don't look back, Deb, only forward, like a thoroughbred at Santa Anita.* "You are your people's hope, your family's dreams," Grandma reminded me.

Though proud of my family's immigrant history, I wanted desperately to shed its legacy of chaotic relationships, mental illness, and alcoholism, like a snake crawling out of its skin. Deliberately living away from home was part of the plan. I was happy with peanut butter on Ritz crackers and washing dishes in the dorm Food Service for free dinners, if it meant the freedom to live in peace among my books, exploring new concepts and a new lifestyle. "Almost there, Deb." Or so I thought.

I saw him across the lobby, leaning forward on the edge of his seat, against a stark white wall decorated with travel posters. It was my father whom I had not seen in years. *Why? Shit! Damien told him! Nice going, Bro!* He was scanning the crowd, expecting a family reunion I wanted no part of. I was the daughter he left behind over a decade ago. After childhood visits to mental hospitals, letters from VA rehabs, and care packets of magazines rather than child support, I honestly felt like I raised him and not vice versa. My siblings and I became little soldiers early on. It built character, I told myself. I could put up with a lot more crap (external stressors my therapist called it) than most Westside coeds.

His image came closer as the group traversed the waxy concrete walkway to baggage claim. His affect appeared vulnerable, even from fifteen feet away, socially awkward perhaps, uncomfortable in his Mervyn's dress shirt and tie. The Florsheim wingtips looked unfamiliar on his feet. Digging one hand in his wrinkled, tan trench coat, the other clutching pink carnations wrapped in cellophane. He was forty-five and lived at home with my abuelos. I was his twenty-two-year-old, self-reliant, levelheaded daughter. I prayed I could glide by like an anonymous traveler, catch our ride at the curb, and disappear onto the 101 north to Palo Alto. He arose and approached me. His tight perm and hazel eyes were both flecked with gray. "Hi, Deb. These are for you. Can we grab a bite to eat in Alum Rock?" "Who is this?" an irritated and rushed Nestor asked me. My disingenuous words tripped over my tongue. "Oh, this is my dad."

Hangtown Is

by Deborah Nevárez-Vivolo

"Hangtown?" my cousin the SF shrink asked me incredulously, his eyes wide in disbelief.

"Prima, go home." To the city of angels, its web of freeways, where hazy sunshine streams through palmas, that line its boulevards named for carpetbaggers and Californios…

Hangtown is home for now. To heal the sick in a very broken world & myself as well.

Hangtown is an ice cream shop front where families take selfies with "George" the stuffed mannequin, swinging above them to and fro like a piñata.

Hangtown: my children called it "Plaskerville," home to apple trees and pumpkin patches. A town of contradictions. Light & dark.

Hangtown is where men in Grateful Dead shirts order tamales from church ladies, Buddhist monks in saffron robes bless the forest and its people each year & blood red MAGA banners wave from white pickup trucks & bronze plaques declare "Nothing happened here in 1895."

A place of shadow and light.

Hangtown is covered in gray clouds or blazing sun. A dichotomy in care of climate change: thunderous storms give birth to verdant dogwoods, apple blossom bright & wind in its cottonwoods sounds like taffeta skirts of parlor dances long ago; its pine-scented air fills my lungs & vistas of endless orchards & prolific vineyards ground me…

Hangtown: I smile at its hues of goldenrod, bittersweet & fiery garnet oak & maple leaves, twirling to the earth like ballerinas & persimmons are sold at roadside stands "on the honor system."

Hangtown is the chirp of a hummer or squirrel each morning and dusk; a balm on my soul…

Hangtown is a Kincaide Queen Anne cottage scene dressed in Christmas snow; "home sweet home" hearths to warm yourself by...where we said our vows amid COVID, I pray in Spanish & the sidewalk abruptly ends.

Joan may have been partly right. There is something dark in those cottages.

A place of shadow and light.

Hangtown is a bruise on Miwok ancestral lands, a revisionist California heritage where the dead know no race & thick with ghosts in need of a place to sleep.

Déjalos. I wish them peace, as I do for myself...

Hangtown is not for the faint of heart, where sons of other shores once awaited their fate on a tree & riddled with the collapsed mines of 49ers, who met their golden dream's end.

Hangtown: its creeks & eaves & local Micky Ds, are home to niños perdidos, lost & awaiting a rehab bed, as indifference looks away.

Hangtown's new gold flows in their veins, a jonesing, a relentless unease, akin to the fever pitch of 1848...leading to new gallows...

Hangtown is a lump in my throat at the sight of a manchild shivering or caught in a skewed state of bliss, walking along Highway 49.

Mijo (my son), where are your people? Go home. This is not your promised land...

Computer Uncommon Cubicle Vultures

BY EDGAR RIDER

Hovering around waiting for prey…
Or for a warm body to leave the terminal space;
Be careful, logout quick, don't leave it open!
Information may be compromised,
Scavengers surround you
Where do they come from?
From the sky, no, a hallway?
Out of nowhere from the parking lot,
To the middle of the room,
A Carcass of data awaits.
Lurking behind the doors…
Into the reference center.
Waiting to strike-
Look behind you;
Scavenging in thin air…
They have landed to take over your computer and revel in their
    new cubicle,
Shut it down or…
Miss your chance to save your privacy.
Identity may be contrived against your liking…
And all of your potential belongings may be hijacked.
Vultures in the Library.

A Lesson Sixty Years in the Making

BY LESLIE ROUNDY

If only I had found my voice earlier in life, I wonder how differently things would have turned out for me. Would my siblings and I have not been afraid to speak up in childhood and beyond? Found the love of my life, married, and had children? Would I have had a more rewarding career and climbed the corporate ladder?

I grew up incredibly shy. It began as a young child and continued into early adulthood. I've never really thought about why, until recently. Maybe it was because I was the last child, and my siblings are seven and ten years older than me. They were well into their teenage years while I was maneuvering grade school. I have no doubt that my many years of body issues were at play. I was shielded by my mom as a young girl, as mothers sometimes do, but reflecting back I can see how her doing things *for* me instead of showing me *how* to do them myself, was, in some ways, a setback rather than a blessing.

I've recalled many times over the years the time my mother, sisters, and I were in a hardware store. I was around seven. I clearly remember that we were standing in front of a display of tools and gadgets, and Mom couldn't find what she was looking for. I saw a man standing a few feet from us, so I approached him and asked him if they carried that item. He said, "Oh, I don't work here." I was so embarrassed and completely mortified. And so it began. I truly believe that incident was the onset of me always holding back, "seen but not heard."

When I left home and ventured out into the world on my own, I was a little more outgoing but still not vocal in sharing my thoughts and opinions. I was always afraid to speak up at work. What if I said something wrong? What if everyone thought my idea was horrible—or even worse, stupid? What would people think of me then? I chose to take what I felt was the safe route and not say anything at all. I was smart and "knew my stuff," but to vocalize it? Not happening. This continued for quite some time.

Fast forward several decades. As it does for all of us, my life was changing in many ways ... caring for my elderly mother who was showing signs of dementia and had come to live with me, feeling overwhelmed both professionally and personally, dealing with challenging family dynamics. I found myself experiencing severe anxiety and panic attacks, and my doctor suggested that I see a therapist. I wasn't keen on the idea at first; however, I knew I didn't want to continue living that way.

I am grateful to have found a wonderful therapist who, in the four years we worked together, helped me to discover that I DO have a voice, one worthy of using. It became much easier to speak up at work. In fact, if my previous manager were here, she would tell you I was far more vocal than she would have liked me to be on some occasions. I can now confidently use my voice to share opinions and thoughts with friends, even though we don't always share the same viewpoint.

So back to if only ... would finding my voice earlier have impacted other areas of my life? Since we can't turn back the hands of time there isn't a way to be certain, but knowing what I know now, I'm sure it would have. In some ways though, it doesn't really matter. To quote C.S. Lewis, "You can't go back and change the beginning, but you can start where you are and change the ending."

The Power of Six Words

BY LESLIE ROUNDY

Feeling alive through expressing my creativity.

Hang on to those six words. I'll come back to them shortly.

This week's writing class assignment puzzled me. No prompt? Egads. What would I write about? One morning I found myself whistling while I was sweeping the floor. (I never thought I'd use those two phrases together in a sentence.) Hmm. Maybe I could write about the history of whistling. Is there even such a thing? I quickly ruled that out and went to my source of trusted information, Google, to search for writing prompts. One suggestion was to write about a daily routine from the perspective of your pet. That could be interesting, maybe only to me, but if I were to write about my cat Tyger's day, 90% of it would be sleeping so not much of a story there. After looking at several lists, one caught my eye: a six-word memoir.

According to an article I found, "When Hemingway was famously challenged by his friends to write a story using only six words, he wrote the following: *For sale: Baby shoes, never worn.* Apparently, he's called it his best work." The idea is for the reader to interpret the words into what they believe to be the story. In Hemingway's example, did a tragic death prevent the baby from ever wearing the shoes, or did the baby grow so quickly that they never fit?

I was intrigued enough to see if I could do this for my assignment. I found a video on YouTube of a woman walking her students through the exercise in five steps:

1. Create a "you" list—what you do, what you like, your feelings. Keep writing for about three minutes.

2. Circle two to three items on your list that inspire you to say more.

3. From those items, select one.

4. Freewrite about it for two minutes.

5. Develop a six-word phrase that captures the essence of what you've written—something about you and what matters to you.

I went through the steps, one by one, and at first, I was a little surprised by how my list was unfolding. But as I began to narrow down the items and expound upon my final word, it was exciting to see the end result.

So back to my six words: *Feeling alive through expressing my creativity.* Yep, that sums me up well. I feel fortunate to have creativity in my soul—writing, watercolor painting, crafting, and even in my garden. It's one of the many blessings I got from my mother. I have fond memories of her exploring *her* creative side—sewing, crafting, needlepointing, and tole painting to name a few. I learned so much from her, something I cherish to this day.

I've been painting with watercolors for about four years. I love how the colors blend to create something magical and oftentimes unintended. When I paint, I go into Zen mode, blocking out everything else in life, even if just for an hour.

Many people may not think of gardening as a creative outlet, but to me it's more than planting colorful flowers and varieties of vegetables, from the common to the "what the heck is this?" I think about the things I can add to give my space personality—water features, whimsical wall art, bird feeders, unique trellises.

Writing is my main creative outlet these days. It has always come somewhat easily to me, whether it was writing an employee email when I was in the corporate world, or now that I'm retired, writing for pure enjoyment. It makes me feel fulfilled and … well, *alive!*

My Strategy

by CLS Sandoval

The lists of finalists had been posted. My coach had spelled my name wrong, so the postings were all incorrect. For this reason, I chose not to pose for a picture in front of the five lists of names where my coach's representation of my name appeared. Though I had corrected my speech and debate coach about the correct spelling of my name all year, I had to go to the ballot table every single tournament to make the correction. My first round of finals included a fourth performance of my informative speech on NicVax—a vaccine to help smokers quit— and my duo interpretation of literature—a truncated version of the play *Southern Girls*—that my duo partner and best friend had found and cut for us to perform. I went to my informative round first. I was second to speak. My excitement over our duo being in finals created some hiccups in my performance that I just couldn't recover from. I was merely a sentence or two into my opening when I said the wrong word, then muttered an um or two. I could feel my neck heating up. It was probably the worst rendition of that speech I had ever spoken. "May I please be excused to my next round?" The judges all nodded.

I picked up my black oral interp binder and headed out of the glass door to the left—the opposite direction of my duo round— to my car. Though my mother's burgundy 1982 Mary Kay Director suit was tight in the waist and my heels were higher than I ever wore other than for competition, I ran until I was in the 1994 Pontiac Grand AM that my nana had earned from Mary Kay and later gifted me. I drove off of Point Loma Nazarene's campus to a nearby cul-de-sac, and smoked a Newport 100, closely watching the clock. My boyfriend at the time and his beautiful female partner from Azusa Pacific University had made it to duo finals as well, and I knew that the Christian National Speech Tournament judges would have a bias for their upbeat, fun *Noah's Ark* duo over mine and my partner's. Ours explored the relationship between my character whose rich, white family employed my partner's character's mother as a maid, revealed that the maid's daughter was my character's secret half-sister, and was in no way upbeat. I thought it was essential that we perform last. I took my last drag, turned over the engine and headed back to the non-smoking campus. I ran to our duo round to catch the end of *The Noah's Ark* sing-songy performance. As I walked into the room, though it was packed, my partner turned her body toward me, furrowing her brow. I could tell she was a bit panicked. As the applause roared for *Noah's Ark*, I said in her ear, "I thought it was important we go last. I would never have missed this." She nodded, took a breath, and our names were called. We took center stage, and started as we always did, with our teaser that ended on my line, written by Shari Bailey, "Mama says: Remember: Nice little girls keep their gloves on. Nice little girls keep their gloves white."

Running Away from Grandma

BY CLS SANDOVAL

I spent every Saturday growing up with my great grandparents. My little sister and I would sit on the stools in front of the little tables that our great grandfather had carved out of wood in his spare retirement time, watching *X-Men, Happy Days, The Twilight Zone, Perry Mason, Wheel of Fortune,* and *Jeopardy*. Sometimes it was just Saturday morning; sometimes it would go later in the evening every now and then, an evening during the week. On one of those Saturday afternoons when mom and dad came to pick us up, I wasn't ready to go. Instead of simply getting into my mother's pink Cadillac, I ran away, as fast as my little legs could take me, thinking that I would somehow outrun the inevitability of going home, outrun the inevitability of being separated from my great-grandparents. My great grandmother ran after me. She was at least 80 years old. She fell. It was my fault. Her bone was broken and her skin bled.

When the cancer had stolen too much of my great-grandfather's independence that he could no longer hide his wife's Alzheimer's, it was time to put my great-grandparents into a nursing home.

"I've always been good to you," Grandma declared, backing me into a corner, her fading blue irises somehow a more intense hue. "You have got to get me out of here! I'll pay you!"

Her offer of money made my throat swell. Her gold wedding ring was the only thing she owned worth any money at all. I looked at the uneven hem of her pink polyester pants, knowing that they had met the same fate as the canary yellow dust ruffle she had been forced to leave behind. She always trimmed them when she thought one side was looking longer than the other.

After my great-grandfather's body could no longer sustain him, even to stay with his love, my great-grandmother walked every day. She walked in a circle around the nursing home. She was looking for her husband. She knew he wouldn't leave her. He would be right back. He must have just gone to the grocery store or perhaps to pick up Kentucky Fried Chicken. She just couldn't remember these days. But she remembered he would never leave her.

When my grandmother's legs were too frail with age and osteoporosis, a femur finally fractured. The bed rest was what really killed her, keeping her from searching for her husband. My tears were grief and joy. Now she knows she's right. Grandpa would never run away from her.

The Mothers by Käthe Kollwitz

BY CLS SANDOVAL

Crowded 'round one another, arms embracing each other, they form an impenetrable barrier around the younger generation. Their image carved from wood, I imagine that inside of that outer rim is a ring of mothers one generation, then one generation younger still. Like the rings that form in a tree trunk, the center must be the youngest generation; the future mothers. Lucky for me, I have three rings around me. Though two of those generations have now passed, my mother still forms a barrier around the barrier I provide to my daughter, and now my husband's mother and grandmother join us.

My Best Friend, Nadine

by Kristine Shell

To say my third-grade year at Madison Elementary in Yakima, Washington was difficult is an understatement. My third-grade year at Madison was, by far, my worst school year ever!

Mrs. Erikson was my third-grade teacher at Madison. She was a big woman, gray-haired, heavy set, and mean. Mrs. Erikson took every subject she taught very seriously. Especially penmanship. And it wasn't long before I realized Mrs. Erikson had no respect for left-handed students who thought they could learn cursive. And, if that wasn't awful enough, I wasn't just left-handed. I was also right-eyed and cross dominant. The worst of the worst!

I bent my left wrist as I wrote, smearing the ink on my penmanship paper. Mrs. Erikson was not happy! So, she built me a "wrist brace" from tongue depressors and adhesive tape. I never sensed Mrs. Erikson was trying to help me with my penmanship. The scowl on her face and the tone of her voice said otherwise.

So, I cried.

And that's when the Black girl who sat at the desk in front of me turned around and whispered, "Don't cry. Please don't cry." Her name was Nadine Morrison, and we became fast friends that day. Third grade, however, was still awful.

The following summer, I asked my mom if I could invite my friend, Nadine, to our house for Saturday. Nadine and I could spend the day playing. Mom said "yes," so I phoned Nadine. The next Saturday, Nadine's mom dropped her off at my house. The sun was shining, and the skies were clear. So, Nadine and I spent most of that Saturday outside. We skipped rope on the sidewalk in front of my house and played tetherball in my backyard. Best Saturday ever!

A few weeks later, I asked my mom if I could invite Nadine to spend another Saturday at my house. And that's when my mom told me that she really liked Nadine, but some of our neighbors weren't comfortable with Nadine's visits. I didn't understand, but I knew my mom had the final say.

Nadine and I went to different junior high schools. We lost track of each other. I graduated from college and accepted a teaching position in Wenatchee, Washington. I was visiting my mom in Yakima one summer weekend when mom told me Nadine Morrison had been a guest speaker at Davis High School's recent graduation ceremony. Mom told me she went to the graduation ceremony to hear Nadine speak. Mom said Nadine's speech as well as her achievements were impressive.

I was happy for Nadine. As an adult, I knew Nadine had overcome more obstacles than I ever had. I felt blessed to have known Nadine Morrison. Heaven knows, at age eight, Nadine Morrison had more smarts and more compassion than many adults have.

Save Me

by Scharlett Stowers Vai

This pain in my heart is slowly killing me.
I will surely die.

BLUE. But I'm not afraid to die.
There's no place to go to be free from this pain.

I CANNOT CRY.

There are no more tears.
I must try to be happy
    and await my fate.

All those who understood are gone now.
I am alone, an alien, unable to go, too...

Now on a journey alone
        SOMEWHERE...
I can be free from this pain.

I'm still waiting; the tears I cry are BLUE, not clear.
No one can see them or see the tracks of those tears.
If you look close into my eyes, you can see them.

I'm drowning in my own tears.

Beware! As you look deeply.
Be careful there — they'll ensnare you.

This pain will overwhelm you
      before you can look away.
Once felt, you'll never be the same.

BEWARE!!! Soooo intense. Soooo deep.
Run away if you can,
      you'll be consumed if you don't.
SAVE YOURSELF!

Note: This prose poem was inspired by my muse Marvin Gaye while
I was listening to his *Vulnerable* album on a blue Sunday afternoon.
His music resonates at a spiritual level... His words are like prayer
for me.

On a Given Weekday

by Heather Takenaga

How can I feel you when
I'm alone this morning?
Your tracks
ripple on the cover.

You must have
tickled my armpits,
yanked my hair,
kicked my shins,
snored in my ear,
stole all the blankets
five times last night.

I try to decipher
your scent in cotton,
this curious language
we share.

My head is cold,
but I can trace
your kiss on my forehead.

Raw

by Heather Takenaga

No parents
No condom
No bed
He eclipses me
over the countertop

We can't
 You want it
We shouldn't
 You need it

My hands trapped
above my head
My eyes on
dinner boiling
on the stove

The noodles
 It's fine
The chicken
 Shut up
We rock

I think
 Is the pot hot enough?

Swath of March

by Heather Takenaga

Winter sneezed over southern California,
my mother's budding daisies & poppies
cotton balled by icy feathers.

Powdery softness prickled
& melted onto my hand,
just like it did when

I once huddled into
the public phone booth that
ate my last quarter to call

my mother, my car frozen on the road.
Frost stung my arms, tickled my teeth,
the receiver frizzled her voice sharp.

We're fine.
Thanks.
Goodbye.

I wondered then,
as I do now,
which was colder.

The Hunt

by Heather Takenaga

Tell us about yourself
> *I am a creative problem-solver*
> who is Isis, an ivory statue
> the destroyer of galaxies
> and reformer of kingdoms
> in my last DnD campaign

Where do you see yourself in five years?
> *I see myself in a position of advancement*
> so I can
> sleep in a bed of my own
> release my deathgrip on my purse
> during the two-hour bus ride to get here
> smile like a dog, less like a shark
> swipe the lint in my jeans with cash

My résumé is like my high school trophies, dusted and forgotten
I shine light on the gold
hoping it glistens, not dim

Thank you for applying
> pressure to the open wound
> because somewhere in there
> my heart is beating,
> pulsing for drops

We'll get back to you
> *You'll hear from us soon*
> *We really appreciate you*
> to land
> somewhere

There's a hunt, and I'll hit a mark
somehow is the spark that keeps me going.

Whew, What a Woman

BY HEATHER TAKENAGA

Eight hours of sleep but no rest
No one to hold her in bed
Sleepers in her eyes
Bag under her chin
Caffeine fingers twitching
Stomach looping knots
Toes blue from slipping on steps
Hair crusted with dried tears & drool
Least her teeth's brushed.

What a woman.

But
she is up.

No ring on her finger
only

rings resonatin' in her heart,
chanting for her to keep rising,
keep strutting, keep laughing,
keep dancing, keep breathing,
keep on doing what it is to
paint the world with a brush that
never sticks to the walls,
swipe the skies,
splash colors on the stars,
repaint the constellations—
don't stop.
Don't stop
until the rings become

what a woman
what a woman
what a woman!

Hummingbirds

BY GUDELIA VADEN

Before the pandemic I was too busy with dancing, ceramics and writing classes. I did not have time to notice hummingbirds buzzing around the bright orange flowers on the Honeysuckle vines in my backyard. The pandemic came in 2020 and brought my outside activities to a screeching halt and isolated me. I knew that a dark cloud of depression would soon follow if I did not find an outlet. One day, my heart fluttered with joy, as I noticed a gray hummingbird with a green tail fly by my kitchen window and flittered off into the teal sky. I wanted more.

My son, Patrick, found out that I liked hummingbirds and gifted me a red hummingbird feeder. My husband, Tom, hung it from a black chain attached to a hook on the patio in front of the kitchen window. I made a special sugar water treat to entice the hummingbirds to visit. I got the recipe from a UCR master gardener. Our yard has lots of Jacaranda trees, flowers and bushes in vivid colors of crimson and fuchsia, perfect for attracting birds and giving them a safe place to nest.

There are many things that fascinate me about hummingbirds. I love their iridescent shades. My favorite are the ruby-throated males. I can hear their humming sounds when it comes close to a flower or bird feeder to feed. Their tiny wings make the sound. That is how they got their name. I enjoy watching closely to see their flight patterns. I thought the hummingbirds were trapeze artists, flying forward, backward and upside down!

Hummingbirds helped me to stay positive and ward off the blues during the lockdown of the pandemic. The pandemic is here to stay and hopefully the hummingbirds are too!

The Accidental Writer

by Gudelia Vaden

My early dreams were to be a movie star as a kid growing up in Planada in the San Joaquin Valley. The movies and our black and white television made movie stars look larger than life. My sisters and I wanted to be the Lennon sisters, as they appeared on *The Ed Sullivan Show*. In the summer under a tent at the park, we viewed movies for ten cents. My friends and I would have fun, as we mimicked Sandra Dee and Debbie Reynolds. They were my role models.

One day my Hollywood aspirations were dashed when I was six years old and a talent scout came and rang my doorbell. That is the closest I ever came to being a movie star. It was surreal that a talent scout came to my small town. The scout wanted to do a screen test. My overprotective father did not allow him past the front door. My dad's face turned crimson as he slammed the screen door. He shouted in a voice so loud it could have broken the sound barrier. There was no way and under no circumstances was he going to agree to a screen test for his daughters. My sisters were four and nine years old.

I have often wondered what could have resulted in that screen test. Father must have had his reasons for his decision. When his mind was made up there was no turning back.

When my dad was five years old living in Canoga Park, he was picked to star in a Charlie Chaplin movie. The movie role called for a charming little boy and my dad fit the script perfectly, so he got the part. He felt that he should have been paid more for his role, though the part was minor. He believed that movie directors exploited and took advantage of young children. The people on the set were nice to my dad and he was glad to have met and worked with Charlie Chaplin. Dad mentioned that Charlie Chaplin was so funny in his baggy pants and mustache that he laughed so loud his stomach ached.

There went my movie aspirations. I spent my time working in schools and only wrote what was essential, such as lesson plans. Then in 1997, I took a class at UCR called "The Exceptional Child." The homework was to write about a social issue that pertained to children. I wrote and illustrated a book called *Natasha's Glasses*, a story about my granddaughter who needed glasses. I never intended to write a book, but felt like this issue should be addressed, as the kids at school called her four eyes and teased her. I received an A. My classmates and professor inquired if I had plans to get it published. Later on, this ignited the spark that inspired me to continue writing.

In 2010, I picked up a copy of the *Pacesetter*, a booklet that offered classes at the Goeske senior center. The booklet fell out of my slippery hands and landed on the page where in black bold letters there were the words, "**Write Your Life Story**!" I thought to myself, is this really what I want to do, write my life story? I showed up on the first day of class, which was a Monday and was accepted. We are The Writing Warriors! Rose, the facilitator, gives us weekly prompts to write our memoirs. I learned so much about myself and about writing. I acquired the confidence needed to contribute to the Inlandia anthology. The great reward is that I have motivated others to write. I am delighted to be writing and have enjoyed the various workshops that Inlandia provides. I feel that writing is probably better than any screen test. It does not matter whether you are a deliberate writer or an accidental writer, but keep on writing.

Pan Dulce de La Nana Pancha

BY FRANCES J. VÁSQUEZ

My maternal ancestors were from Sonora, a northern state in México where the geography is diverse and contains a vast swath of the unique Sonoran Desert and includes majestic cathedrals of the Sierra Madre Mountains. Below the mountains and volcanoes lay immense fertile valleys. The climate is arid and sweltering hot in northwestern Sonora most of the year especially during summer, spring, and fall. Winters are mild with ever hopes of rain, similar to Inland Southern California winters. The indigenous inhabitants of the terrain are the resilient Yoeme-Yaqui ethnic peoples who live and thrive with the opportunities and challenges of their environment.

Sonora valleys are conducive to agriculture due to the fertile sandy loam soil of *el Valle del Río Yaqui*, coupled with life-giving water from two large rivers, Río Yaqui and Río Mayo, and their tributary canals, along with vital irrigation from a large dam, *Presa Alvaro Obregón*. The Río Yaqui Valley has the best and most extensive agricultural irrigation system in México. The land produces an abundant cornucopia of various crops to feed Mexicans and for exportation: fruits, vegetables and legumes, and multiple types of grains (wheat, soy, alfalfa, etc.).

My grandmother Francisca Valenzuela Burboa was born to a family of bakers from Batacosa in the Quiroga region of Sonora in México. Her parents, José Maria Valenzuela and Rosa Burboa owned and operated a prosperous panadería — a neighborhood bakery.

During the Mexican Revolution (1910 – 1920), the Valenzuela-Burboa family moved to Esperancita a small agricultural settlement about six kilometers from la Divina Providencia, a *pueblito en el Valle del Río Yaqui* where they eventually stayed. Providencia is a small village a few kilometers outside Ciudad Obregón, a medium-size city in the Cajeme District where my Grandmother established an adobe home and where my Mother Rosa Lidia was born. This is where "La Nana Pancha" (as she was endearingly called in her village) lived and practiced her profession as a Partera (midwife), Yerbera (herbalist), and Curandera (folk healer).

With the help of her son José María Paredes Valenzuela (Tío Chemali), Nana maintained a 26-hectare *Ejido* of farm land where they cultivated tall, verdant wheat crops. Nana's tierras were near Campo Trés where Tío Chemali and his wife, Refugio Pablos (Tía Cuca) lived with their five children: Maria Eugenia, Jesus Armando, Rosa Maria, Francisca, and Guadalupe. For many years they maintained a farm adjacent to a large canalón (canal) where we often swam.

I recall playing in a large concrete storeroom at Campo Trés where my Tío stored gunny sacks full of plump wheat grains. The storeroom was attached to their family home. Using the wheat grain grown on her own farm lands, my Nana baked whole-wheat bread, rolls, and pan dulce in an outdoor earthen oven in the backyard patio of her home.

In addition to Nana's renown as a proficient midwife and folk healer, she gained fame as a consummate baker. The aroma of fragrant, freshly baked bread easily transports me to childhood visits with my grandmother in Providencia. The windowless bedroom where my mother, sisters, and I slept in was converted into a prep room during Nana's occasional baking sprees. This was where the yeast dough leavened. A large Yaqui-style woven cowhide bed served to support trays of dough while the bolitas (balls) rested overnight to rise in preparation for baking.

I wish I had a photo of Nana taking out her aromatic and delectable baked goods from her traditional earthen oven. I can readily transport to yesteryear and imagine my Nana opening the black wrought iron door of her adobe horno. It was located at the rear of the patio by a Carrizo (dry reed) fence. The mound-shaped horno was made of the same bronze tierra as Nana's adobe home. The veneer of the horno resembled a smooth caramel brown plaster.

I delight in imagining Nana's face beaming with satisfaction for having completed an arduous and time-consuming task, for she would have formed bolitas and filled some of the bolitas with fruit fillings ahead of baking day. On baking day, she would have risen before dawn to fire up the wood-burning horno.

Using a flat shovel-like wooden paddle, I can see Nana taking out a dozen or more perfectly baked *Coyotas*, a popular sweet specialty of the region. The edges of the round flaky cookies are browned a few shades brighter than the rest of the baked goods. The Coyotas are filled with local fruits at hand: biznaga (barrel cactus), tamarindo, calabaza, camote, guayaba, and panocha. She also made fruit filled empanadas. Among Nana's favorites were Cemitas (large round seeded buns) which were baked plain — ideal for dipping into cups of hot café.

I imagine her eyes feeling weary after laboring for a long morning to beat the hot Sonoran Sun. Her long, straight black hair, usually fashioned smoothly in a chongo (bun) at the nape of her neck, has loosened. Stray hairs drape over her forehead, which is blistered with droplets of perspiration. Regardless, she looks happy with the satisfaction of knowing she is about to give away the finest products of her bountiful wheat harvest.

Smiling, I envision Nana packing her freshly baked delicacies to gift to friends and relatives in Cócorit, an historical and magical town where my cousin Panchi fondly talks about her accompanying our Nana to give away cardboard boxes filled with empanadas, coyotas, cemitas, and other baked goods for annual Días de Muertos festivities at the ancient Cócorit cemetery.

"*¡Wepa! Wepa! Vengan a comer!*" La Nana de Providencia would shout out joyfully as she stood at her front door beckoning neighbors and passers-by to come inside and eat… a welcomed invitation for lucky recipients to enjoy Doña Pancha's delectable pan dulce con café.

Café de Talega

by Frances J. Vásquez

I was allowed to stay for short periods of time with Tía Cuca and my five cousins, especially when my Tío Chemali was in México City on business. They lived at Campo Trés where they grew vegetable crops near their home. They also grew sizable wheat and other grain crops nearby at their *Ejido*. I enjoyed being at Campo Trés because I got to play with my cousins: Maria Eugenia, Jesus Armando, Rosa Maria, Francisca, and Guadalupe.

During my Campo Trés overnight visits, Tía Cuca served me a cup of *café con leche* with breakfast in the morning. I enjoyed the warm sweet beverage. The café was like a latte: brewed coffee diluted with generous dashes of Carnation evaporated milk and sweetened with ample spoonfuls of brown sugar. I noticed that my Tía brewed her café in a dark enamel-speckled metal coffee pot into which she placed a *talega* [made of an elongated *manta* cone cotton filter which was sewn along a round metal rim to suspend over a coffee brewing vessel], into which she added ground coffee. Tía then poured hot water into the *talega* to brew the beverage. Eventually, I learned that this ancient coffee-brewing process is unique to the northern Mexican states of Sonora and Baja California — it is called "Café de Talega."

One bright spring day while visiting with my Nana Francisca, we happened to be alone — a rare happening. She beckoned me to follow her as she wanted to show me how to roast raw coffee beans. This would be the first and only time that I would observe Nana's traditional process of roasting *café al estilo Sonorense* (Sonora-style coffee roast). I am fortunate and proud for Nana having shown me this ancient culinary tradition when I was a child.

Nana took down a wide, shallow *cazuela de barro* that hung on her kitchen wall. The ancient terracotta roasting pan was shiny ebony black on the inside. The outside was scorched black from the searing flames of many fires. She lit firewood on a brazier outdoors in the patio until the logs were red hot and had begun to ashen. She placed the cazuela on the logs to heat until it was blazing hot. She sprinkled handfuls of raw coffee beans onto the heated cazuela. Using a sturdy wooden spoon, she stirred the beans constantly until they toasted to a rich obsidian color. After this process, she gradually stirred in handfuls of crumbled *piloncillo* (brown sugar) onto the toasted beans to caramelize the sugar until the mixture turned into a thick shiny black paste that bubbled and crackled. Nana swiftly spooned the gooey black globs onto a large metal sheet and rapidly flattened and smoothed the mixture to cool and harden. After the café/sugar mixture hardened, it looked as if it were an obsidian nut candy brittle. Nana deftly broke up the dense café brittle into small pieces and ground them in an old metal hand-drawn *molino* (coffee mill).

Back in the USA, I didn't drink coffee again until I was in my late teens. My family brewed it using a percolator process and served it with canned evaporated milk. As an adult, I began to drink my brew black — no sugar or milk. I am somewhat of a coffee connoisseur and buy whole coffee beans to grind each morning for my daily cup of café. I use a "pour-over" brewing process with an individual Mellita filter which I place on top of my favorite mug dedicated to coffee. I like my café freshly brewed and HOT. Occasionally, I brew it with a cinnamon stick to impart a distinctive, aromatic flavor. I favor the "pour-over" process for its simplicity, which also meets my health and aesthetic preferences. According to a news article I read many years ago, we derive the best health benefits from coffee when consumed within 20 minutes after brewing.

Special acknowledgement to ancient Ethiopian civilizations for originally cultivating the coffee plants in the Kaffa province. And, kudos to the Arabian culture for creating a pivotal roasting process to make the beans suitable for human consumption. The *Cafea Arabica* beans produce my favorite café beverage — one I enjoy daily. I am grateful that coffee beans were brought to México centuries ago where a variety of plant species thrive in climate-specific regions. Of course, Mexicanos developed innovative ways to prepare the café and added their own special and regional flair to the beverage, like the ancestral Café de Talega brewing process developed by the indigenous of Sonora hundreds of years ago.

The Mexican Revolution in the 20th century inspired *soldaderas* and *Adelitas* to prepare *Café de Olla* in the soldier camps when they were out fighting the war — literally — coffee on the run. Into a large cooking vessel (usually terracotta), they simply placed water, coffee grounds, and *piloncillo* (raw sugar cones) — and if available, spices like cinnamon sticks, cloves, and star anise. Over a log fire they boiled the ingredients altogether and after the grounds settled to the bottom, they served the café beverage hot into cups for the soldiers to energize and sustain them. Café brewed in a terracotta olla imparts a subtle earthy flavor and aroma — giving it a uniquely Mexican flair.

If I could journey back in time, I would ask my Nana to give me one of her whole wheat Coyotas de Guayaba and another of Biznaga. After savoring these wholesome delicacies, I would ask Tía Cuca for a cup of her aromatic Café de Talega — straight, no flavorings. Heaven!

¡Viva Café de Talega!

The Company That Changed My Life

BY JOSE VIZCARRA

In my life I have learned many good, useless, great, and indifferent lessons that have made an impact in my life. There is one company that I feel has changed the most powerful industry in North America and my life: Primerica. Why has this company changed my life? So many people receive the elementary, secondary, and higher education that takes years to complete, and yet personal finance education is not existent. I was a victim of my own deficient financial education for many years until I received the best education in my life.

It all started when I was working in two jobs as a teacher to support my family as a single parent with two children. The financial pressure that most people feel creates in us stress and mental conditions of giving up. One day I picked up a newspaper and read the wanted ads for jobs. One in particular caught my attention, about a part time opportunity to earn extra income. I drove to the North Hollywood office from my apartment in Los Angeles. I did not know what to expect. I had had several jobs before I completed my teacher´s preparation to work in a school. My lack of financial education hurt my family. I was clueless about money and how to use it because the dollar bills did not have any instructions on how to use them. As I walked into the office I was met by the man who placed the ad in the newspaper. He welcomed me into the meeting that evening.

There the speakers began to show us some powerful concepts that I had been ignorant about, like the Rule of 72 that is used to double the money at a specific interest rate and how the interest rate on loans can double the debt in a few years. I wondered why the schools did not teach such important rules. The speaker talked to us about a crusade to fight the most corrupt industry in the country, life insurance, which is so important and yet so many people do not believe or care. I was happy to have it, but to my surprise the school district only provided $5,000 in life insurance benefits. I was excited to have attended such an incredible meeting. They educated me about investing money and time to acquire wealth for my retirement. I had never been exposed to such powerful information that I felt everyone should learn. My excitement grew when they mentioned that I could have a business. They mentioned that it was better to join on a part-time basis, rather than going full-time right away. I loved how they prepared the people who joined to become a broker, go full-time and own a business that we could sell or that our loved ones could inherit.

I joined the business that day and I am still actively searching for clients and people who want to increase their income. The feeling that I can help so many people inspires me to educate families who have never been taught these important facts.

When they asked me about my salary, which was higher than the normal worker's salary, I felt proud until the presenter asked me how much money I had at the end of the month. The cruel reality is that it does not matter how much you make; what counts is how much you have at the end of the month. I learned to eliminate all debt that so many people suffer from. I was one of those people who did not have control of my spending.

Other lessons about being a business owner caught my attention because I had never thought about having my own business. I knew that to have a business, capital was required, and I did not have any idea what business I wanted to have. The leader explained that the only capital needed was to apply for a license that would cost $60 and I would become a 1099 during the tax season. I could not believe that I could pay less taxes on my income by claiming business expenses.

My life changed when I was able to control my own future by locating leaders who want to build their own businesses. They showed me that the starting income was $250 or more an hour of my part-time effort on top of what I earned in my career. Most businesses have many expenses while this business was only $25 a month to run my business. It was the passion to help and educate people who had never been exposed to the most important education in life.

The End

BY KARA WORRELLS

The sky will swallow you whole one day.
Each limb
will be ripped from each socket and
a river of blood will flow.

Your body, no more. And
what will be left of you?
Your fingerprints on the lives you've touched?
Your footprints in the fresh cement of birth?

The violence does not pick and choose.
We suffocate, we perish, we break.
Whether we are awake or not
is exhaustion.

Crocheting for My Grandmother

BY KARA WORRELLS

To crochet is to live with you again
in the embrace of seven not yet eight.
> Memory embraces you seven times,
> wearing four different aprons again.
Aprons for cooking meals, never again
tasted. I cook your recipes alone.
> Mamá's green thumb harvests for recipes.
> She mixes like you while I watch alone.
She chef. She artist. She mother. She cares.
I crochet your motherhood in the now
> to prevent more attempts. I live now
> in the attempt of making something new
from the template of you that lives in me.
To crochet is to live with you again.

The People Study: A Patch Named Kara

by Kara Worrells

There are words I can't decipher.
This critical mind. These senses.
The stick-and-poke of day.
        I paint myself nature.
Is that what I'm meant to do?
Stop awareness? Stop seeing?
Stop hearing? Just be?
I can't. It's outside of me.
        Ink of earth I sit in.
Blades of grass
that Whitman questioned
in a single baby's breath.
I listen and look into questions.
        See dots of green and red.
Finally free of the selves?
They groan about in the No Exit hell
of jealousy enraged. The people.
Their tone. Their misunderstanding.
Their grief and pain.
        Spilling guts onto grass.
What does it mean to be free?
I don't know them.
They don't know me.
They won't even stop if I do.
        There are words I can't decipher.
Why do they want me to sleep?
What did I do? What is wrong with
observing in silence?
        These senses affect me.

Contributor Bios

Janet Lako Alexander is a poet, writer, and bilingual educator. A UC Riverside graduate, she was born in Blythe and raised in Rubidoux, California. Her works have appeared in *Writing from Inlandia* and other publications. She teaches poetry writing/performance for the Ontario-Montclair School District.

Mary Briggs is a first-generation Mexican American. She was born in 1939 to a family of migrant workers and raised in East Los Angeles. Mary has resided in Riverside since 1991.

Stephanie Bruce has written songs and poems all her life. Eight years ago, she expanded her writing into short stories, fiction, and non-fiction. She says whether it's writing fiction, non-fiction, poetry, or song...putting heart to pen and pen to paper is a magical process. One that she enjoys daily.

Georgette Geppert Buckley: Amidst combatting diagnosis with diet and supplements, exercise, and prayer Georgette Geppert Buckley concocted an amazing gluten-free gingerbread and learned to write (paint) Byzantine Icons. With her daughters, she hiked Mt. Rubidoux. In this anthology, Georgette offers short shorts (not cutoffs) and one short poem and is forever indebted to Wil and the Celena Scribes group.

Bridgette Callahan has lived in the Inland Empire for thirty-five years, where she earned various degrees at Riverside Community College and California State University, San Bernardino. She has been teaching writing at the University of Redlands for eleven years, and her writing has appeared in *Pacific Review* and *The Beacon*.

Ellen Davidson Cantor uses poetry to interpret her feelings and to examine how events impact her life. Ellen received a BS from The University of Illinois at Champaign-Urbana and continued her education in Interior and Architectural Design at UCLA. She has studied poetry through Inlandia and with Nancy Woo.

Alben Chamberlain is a retired public school teacher, retirement counselor, federal bank examiner, and US Navy Reserve officer. He graduated from San Bernardino Valley College, Brigham Young University-Hawaii, and The American Graduate School in Glendale, Arizona. He is married and has three grown children and four grandchildren to spoil. He has lived most of his life in the Inland Empire region and somehow survived.

Natalie Champion participated in the Chronologyland workshop. She is a poet and kindergarten teacher. She is from the Inland Empire but lives in San Francisco with her husband Rick and cat Milo Morris.

Rick Champion self publishes a Zine, *Natalie's Zine*, which is described as "A San Francisco Home for Artists and Writers." Included in the Zine are Chronologies – stories and poems – as well as drawings, photography – both contemporary and historical – and murals by street artists. The youngest contributor is seven years old. The oldest contributor is ninety-one.

Sylvia Clarke finds blessings in listening to stories and poetry by others in the Inlandia workshops she attends: Writing Warriors led by Rose Monge and Celena's Scribes facilitated by Wil Clarke. They inspire her to share her own writings.

Wil Clarke is looking forward to publishing his memoir on five years spent in Tanzania, East Africa. He enjoys participating in Rose Monge's Memoir Writing Workshop and facilitating Celena's Scribes Workshop. He grew up in Africa and has lived in Riverside for three dozen years.

James Coats is a poet, performer, and educator born in Los Angeles and raised in the Inland Empire. With a passion for all things creative, he strives to capture authentic self-expression through his imagistic narrative poetry. You can find him attending poetry readings throughout California or follow him on Instagram @ MrLovingWords.

Elinor Cohen wanted to be an astronomer but couldn't commit to all the math. So instead she got a degree in Pre-Modern Literature that she never uses. Elinor resides with her family in the desolate desert after decades as an Angeleno and is fully obsessed with her rescue dog Floof.

Chuck Doolittle has been a member of The Joslyn Joy Writers in Redlands for nearly three years. He is a retired teacher who enjoys spending free time writing and volunteering. He relishes the creative expression that both prose and poetry present. Mainly, he just enjoys writing.

Reiss DuPlessis is a retired State of California employee. He writes for fun and to share his memories with the next generations of his family.

Jerry Ellingson lives in Redlands, California. Her goal is to record family stories so her genealogy work will not only have photos and statistics, but stories that should be told. She is a retired teacher with a Bachelor's degree in Dance and English. Her Master's degree is in Education. The greatest joys in her life have been teaching Graphic Design and Computers to adults and her role as a mother and grandmother.

Eric Epstein is an ASL poet whose work has been featured in the Folger Shakespeare Library traveling exhibition and the *Rail Switch* journal. He has presented at various colleges and libraries about sign language poetics. His groundbreaking curriculum on ASL poetry can be found in his online course signplaying.com.

Bryan Franco is a neurodivergent, gay, Jewish poet from Brunswick, Maine. He is published in the US, Australia, England, Germany, Holland, India, Ireland, and Scotland, hosts Café Generalissimo open mic, and is an artist and culinary genius. His book *Everything I Think Is All in My Mind* was published in 2021.

Nan Friedley is a retired special education teacher and graduate of Ball State University, Muncie, Indiana. Her piece "Three," is a nonfiction anthology collection published in Push Pen Press. She has participated in various workshops sponsored by Inlandia.

Camille Gaon is a lover of anything literary and unleashes her imagination daily to indulge in unsubdued storytelling. She has written and performed pieces at The Wallis Annenberg Center for Performing Arts in Beverly Hills and at The Broad Stage in Santa Monica even though she can't act.

Ragini Goel has a Master's degree in Sanskrit and a teacher's degree in English. People who know Ragini describe her as a Renaissance woman with varied interests. Ragini is an appointed commissioner with the Human Relations Council. Ragini says her best achievements are her two sons Sumeet and Amit.

Milan Hamilton is a retired nonprofit executive and educator who loves poetry and is a member of the Academy of American Poets. He has written blogs about his life and experience, including photography.

Dora Harmon cree lo que define su personalidad es fé, positivismo y fortaleza y piensa que las tragedias que vivimos son solo enseñansas que nos toca a aprender y agradeser, porque las de ellas solo han logrado dejar en su corazón fé, fortaleza y riqueza interior. Ella falicita dos clubs de lectura.

Connie Jameson, a retired elementary and special education teacher, enjoys reading, writing, travel, nature, antiques, theater, and Toastmasters. Her first published book was *Dating 'n' Mating: Wit and Wisdom on Love and Marriage*. Connie recently published her first children's picture book, *Twinkle Toes*.

Margo Klein is a retired CPA. She joined Joslyn Joy Writers at the urging of a friend and found the love of writing.

Robin Longfield began writing poetry almost as soon as she learned to put a pencil on paper. Her work has appeared in several journals and anthologies. She is grateful for the support of her family and friends. She still believes in magic, possibilities, and adventures.

Merrill Lyew is retired. After graduating, he stayed in the academic world for a decade. Thereafter he worked at a private company until retirement. His job required traveling to the metropolitan areas of Latin America. These trips were eventful, some of which might be the theme of his short stories.

Anne Malcolm holds a BSc in Plant Sciences from UC Riverside. She immigrated to America in the mid 1980's from England. Her childhood was spent in East Africa. She has an international perspective, and feels lucky to have landed in Redlands; a safe, sunny paradise in which to raise her children. Anne is grateful to Mae Wagner Marinello and the Joywriters for creating a safe place for writing and sharing her autofiction.

Shannon Malloy is a neurodivergent poet exploring themes of body horror and dysfunction, abuse, and acceptance. Her unique perspective delves deep into the intricacies of human experience. Her work examines the dark and often taboo aspects of living inside a broken psyche and body. Shannon grew up in Nebraska and now resides in Denver.

Mae Wagner Marinello has been a part of Inlandia since 2008. She began facilitating a weekly workshop at the Joslyn Senior Center in Redlands in 2014. When the pandemic hit, the Joslyn Joy Writers never missed a beat, meeting weekly via Zoom. They continue as a hybrid group with some writers attending in person and some attending via Zoom from as far away as Ireland and Arkansas. Mae is a mother of three, grandmother of nine, and great-grandmother of seven. She lives in Redlands with her joyful little dog named Cricket.

Elisse Martinez was born in Buffalo, NY, and moved to Riverside in 1970 with her family. She received her Master of Education at Hunter College and her Special Ed Credential from UCR. Elisse came to writing at the age of 80, inspired by Renee Gurley's Show Us! Don't Tell Us! writing classes.

Rose Y. Monge has facilitated the memoir group at the Goeske Center since 2009. She believes that writing a memoir is therapeutic and healing for the writer and educational and inspirational for the reader. Her memoir honors her parents' devotion to their children. She advocates social justice, diversity, and inclusion in the community.

Maury Mortensen is semi-retired from hotel and resort management occupations. However, since childhood, he has had a penchant for writing what he calls "ditties" Give him a subject or information about a person, and in a short time, he will have a rhyming Ditty for you, and he will write a cute rhyming poem.

Barbara Mortensen, an active senior, retired from a career in international corporate management and a second career as an adjudicator for the State of California. She has served on many charity boards and is an activist for women's and other civil rights. Her love of music led her to be the driving force in bringing the Metropolitan Opera live simulcast to the greater Palm Springs area. She is a published writer of memoirs and incidental biographical essays. She is a foodie and has met a few meals she didn't like. She lives with her husband and a houseful of rescue dogs and cats.

Cindi Neisinger is a coffeeholic and the co-writer of *Sunny Sund: The Woman Behind Don the Beachcomber, Inc. - A Hollywood Story*. Her current work-in-progress is titled *You're Muted*, the first book in her ZoomLandia Series. Additionally, she is working on her memoir, *My Life Between a Tortilla and White Bread*.

Deborah Nevárez-Vivolo is a Chicana who was born and raised in East Los Angeles, a UCLA graduate, mother of three adult sons, and a breast cancer survivor. She resides in California's Sierra foothills, serves the community as a psychotherapist, and is currently writing a family memoir.

Edgar Rider wrote this poem under the nom de plume Bob Eager. He regularly uses the pseudonym Eager to describe situations that are a bit more abstract and situations that have unusual subject matter.

Leslie Roundy is a resident of Redlands, California, and has enjoyed writing with the Joslyn Joy Writers and Inlandia Institute workshops. Now that she is retired, Leslie is pursuing her passion for writing more creatively. She also volunteers with the senior centers in Redlands, where she is president of the Senior Activities Advisory Board and writes a monthly e-newsletter.

CLS Sandoval, PhD (she/her) is a pushcart nominated writer and communication professor accomplished in film, academia, and creative writing who performs, writes, signs, and rarely relaxes. CLS is raising her daughter, son, and dog with her husband in Walnut, CA.

Kristine Shell lives in Redlands, California, where she participates in the Joslyn Writers Group and the Inlandia Institute. Kristine is a retired school administrator and teacher. She holds Bachelor of Arts degrees in English and Secondary Education. She also holds Master of Education degrees in Elementary Reading and School Administration. Kristine has been with the Inlandia Institute since October 2016.

Scharlett Stowers Vai is a lifelong resident of Casa Blanca and is a Brown Beret and activist for la Causa. She is bilingual and biliterate in English and Spanish. She participated in the Tesoros de Cuentos creative writing workshops with Frances J. Vásquez at the SSgt. Salvador J. Lara Casa Blanca Library.

Heather Takenaga (her/she) is a writer and poet. Born and raised in Riverside, CA. Currently writing short stories and poetry. Drooling for cat cuddles, bedtime snuggles, and a reading vacation.

Gudelia Vaden (Delia), is a teacher, poet, writer, and artist. Her writings reflect her love of nature and writing. She illustrates and contributes to Natalie's Zine, an online magazine. While teaching, she earned a BA Degree from California State University, San Bernardino.

Frances J. Vásquez facilitates Tesoros de Cuentos creative writing workshops where her motto is "Palabras Vuelan; los Escritos Quedan | Words Fly; Writings Endure." She is passionate about Chicana/o history and celebrating cultural programs. She serves as Director Emerita of Inlandia Institute and ardently supports its programming and events.

Jose Luis Vizcarra has participated in the Inlandia family of writers for several years. It has developed many writers to reach the highest levels to publish our work of a powerful message. He continues to participate in two classes to develop his style and passion. Every published author would live forever through written words.

Kara Worrells is also known as Kara Worrells-Gutiérrez. Latin@. Queer. Wom@n of letters. A dialectical thinker hailing from Kumeyaay land in California. A dual citizen. An in-betweener. Also known as K, professionally. Or G, personally.

About Inlandia Institute

Inlandia Institute is a regional literary non-profit and publishing house. We seek to bring focus to the richness of the literary enterprise that has existed in this region for ages. The mission of the Inlandia Institute is to recognize, support, and expand literary activity in all of its forms in Inland Southern California by publishing books and sponsoring programs that deepen people's awareness, understanding, and appreciation of this unique, complex and creatively vibrant region.

The Institute publishes books, presents free public literary and cultural programming, provides in-school and after school enrichment programs for children and youth, holds free creative writing workshops for teens and adults, and boot camp intensives. In addition, every two years, the Inlandia Institute appoints a distinguished jury panel from outside of the region to name an Inlandia Literary Laureate who serves as an ambassador for the Inlandia Institute, promoting literature, creative literacy, and community. Laureates to date include Susan Straight (2010-2012), Gayle Brandeis (2012-2014), Juan Delgado (2014-2016), Nikia Chaney (2016-2018), and Rachelle Cruz (2018-2020).

To learn more about the Inlandia Institute, please visit our website at www.InlandiaInstitute.org.

Inlandia Books

Writing from Inlandia annual anthology series

Guajira, the Cuba girl by Zita Arocha

Breaking Pattern by Tisha Marie Reichle-Aguilera

Exit Prohibited by Ellen Estilai

These Black Bodies Are…, edited by Romaine Washington

Vermillion Speedateer by Sebraé Harris

Pretend Plumber by Stephanie Barbé Hammer

Ladybug by Nikia Chaney

Vital: The Future of Healthcare, edited by RM Ambrose

Güero-Güero: The White Mexican and Other Published and Unpublished Stories by Dr. Eliud Martínez

A Short Guide to Finding Your First Home in the United States: An Inlandia anthology on the immigrant experience

Care: Stories by Christopher Records

San Bernardino, Singing, edited by Nikia Chaney

Facing Fire: Art, Wildfire, and the End of Nature in the New West by Douglas McCulloh

In the Sunshine of Neglect: Defining Photographs and Radical Experiments in Inland Southern California,1950 to the Present by Douglas McCulloh

Henry L. A. Jekel: Architect of Eastern Skyscrapers and the California Style by Dr. Vincent Moses and Catherine Whitmore

Orangelandia: The Literature of Inland Citrus edited by Gayle Brandeis

While We're Here We Should Sing by The Why Nots

Go to the Living by Micah Chatterton

No Easy Way: Integrating Riverside Schools - A Victory for Community by Arthur L. Littleworth

www.ingramcontent.com/pod-product-compliance
Lightning Source LLC
Chambersburg PA
CBHW050357030726
47503CB00006B/1898